Mastering Content Generation

Mastering Content Generation

How to Write Quickly and Build a Rich Marketing Content Library

Paula Heikell

ISBN: 1534696164
ISBN 13: 9781534696167

Table of Contents

Introduction

As Marcus Sheridan, founder of The Sales Lion and the creator of a million-dollar business has so famously said, "Great content is the best sales tool in the world."

Most marketers will agree, but they'll quickly tell you that generating good content is a constant challenge, because today's buyers expect to find detailed information online, and they want it to be updated and fresh. All the time.

Before the Internet, companies had much more control over what information they provided to buyers, and when. Now, we as buyers can go online at any time and choose what we want to see and when we want to see it. We can see practically anything and everything that is written about a company or its products, whether it's produced by the company itself, the media, employees posting their own content or customers.

With so much access to information, buyers now have the power to take over the buying cycle on their own terms, because they can go online and make an informed buying decision on their own, without even speaking to a salesperson. It's not surprising that many marketing experts call this the "age of the consumer."

A recent *Forbes* article noted, "Research from Google and CEB titled *The Digital Evolution in B2B Marketing* provides new insight into buyer behavior, and it challenges the conventional wisdom. According to the study, customers reported to being nearly 60 percent through the sales process before engaging a sales rep, regardless of price point. More accurately, 57 percent of the sales process just disappeared."[1]

When these statistics were first published, you could hear a collective large "gulp" from sales and marketing professionals accustomed to the old days of advertising and selling. How on earth could any company hope to promote itself at the right place and time – in a world where the customer is driving the process?

---

1   Scott Gillum, "The Disappearing Sales Process," Forbes.com, Jan. 7, 2013.

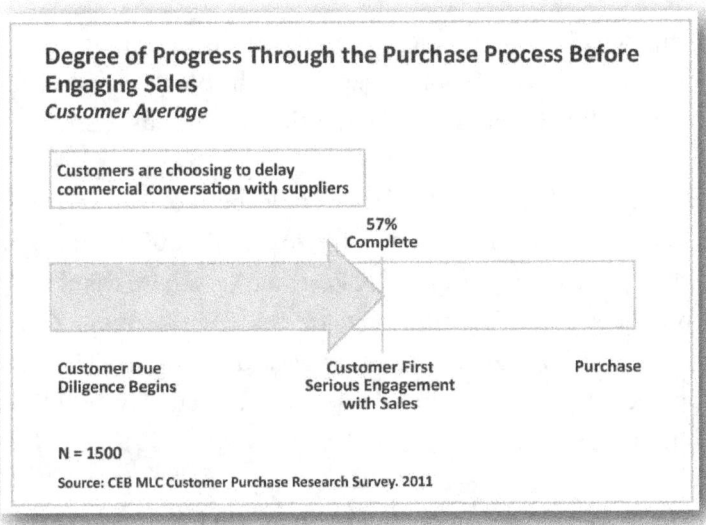

Degree of Progress Through the Purchase Process Before Engaging Sales
Customer Average

Customers are choosing to delay commercial conversation with suppliers

57% Complete

Customer Due Diligence Begins

Customer First Serious Engagement with Sales

Purchase

N = 1500

Source: CEB MLC Customer Purchase Research Survey. 2011

If this tremendous shift in the buyer/seller relationship made some marketers nervous, others saw the competitive edge they could gain by writing good content.

Marketing expert and author Stan Smith, says it well:

> Blogs are the marketing "equalizer" that I've searched for my entire career. Until recently, marketing was a game that only large and rich companies could play. Companies would purchase million dollar commercials during popular TV shows and run commercials to tell their story. The same deep-pocket economics applied to magazine, radio, and billboard advertising. The company with the most

money often won which means that most businesses suf-focated under piles of marketing cash. Blogs correct this inequality, leveling the playing field for all businesses.

"Leveled the playing field." What could be more powerful? The reality is that you no longer have to be the 800-pound gorilla in your industry to win the greatest market share, thanks to the way buyers go online and look for content like blogs to make buying decisions. Any company, regardless of size, is now in a position to reach a much larger buyer group by building an Internet presence.

However, getting out there is one thing. What you say once you're out there will make or break your business. Today's buyers are look-ing for useful information that meets their needs, not your com-pany's needs. Welcome to the world of content-based marketing.

SO, WHAT, EXACTLY, IS CONTENT MARKETING?

We hear the phrase "content marketing" a lot these days, but what exactly does it mean? Here's a good definition from the Content Marketing Institute: "Content marketing is a strategic marketing approach focused on creating and distributing valuable, relevant, and consistent content to attract and retain a clearly-defined au-dience — and, ultimately, to drive profitable customer action."[2]

---

2 "What is Content Marketing?" http://contentmarketinginstitute.com/what-is-content-marketing/ Content Marketing Institute, part of Z Squared Media, LLC, headquartered in Cleveland, Ohio.

It's a method of engaging and informing buyers on their terms to win their trust and loyalty to your brand or product. It's a method of using promotional and non-promotional content to thoughtfully engage buyers on their timelines and their terms.

It marks a very clear transition from creating blatant self-promotional content to creating content that is designed to inform and persuade. This shift that can be hard to make, but it pays off. Well-conceived marketing content can result in more sales leads from new and existing customers than conventional marketing strategies.

I've worked with companies both before and after they adopted content marketing to build business, and the results are amazing. It doesn't happen overnight, but the growth in lead generation and brand awareness is measurable.

WHAT MAKES AN EFFECTIVE CONTENT MARKETING STRATEGY?

To be effective, a content marketing plan is based on a steady stream of targeted content. It is content that is engaging, imminently sharable and, most of all, focused on helping customers to discover (on their own) that your product or service is the one that will scratch their itch.[3]

---

3 Robert Rose and Joe Pulizzi, *Managing Content Marketing: The Real-World Guide for Creating Passionate Subscribers to Your Brand,* CMI Books, 2011.

Comic by Suparno Chaudhuri

Effective content marketing also requires, well, much more content than companies had been accustomed to producing for marketing purposes. Not surprisingly, their traditional pool of writing resources can no longer keep up with the volume of fresh content that's required to stay ahead of the competition and keep buyers engaged. As a result, they're drawing on marketing managers, product managers, sales staff, engineers and others to contribute as writers – whether these new "content generators" feel prepared to write or not.

Whether you're a professional writer looking for content marketing tips, or you're a non-writer who has "inherited" the responsibility to write content, this book is for you. You'll find practical advice to help you start generating content quickly, as well as writing tips to make the process easier and the outcome better. You'll also find practical guidance to avoid common assumptions that lead to weak content and disappointing results.

I hope you find the tips I've provided here to be helpful.

One

Getting Started

"Content marketing is like a first date. If all you do is talk about yourself, there won't be a second date."

— DAVID BEEBE

Where to begin? Many of today's marketers are well aware of the power of content marketing, yet cite that they are lacking in sufficient 1) content, 2) time, or 3) general know-how to launch ongoing content-based marketing campaigns.

This chapter will help you determine how much material you already have to work with and home in on who your audience(s) are. If you take the time to establish these two cornerstones, you'll find it much easier to quickly start producing effective content. Skip these steps, and you can still produce content – but it may not be as well directed or effective in winning customers as you planned.

STEP 1: IDENTIFY YOUR AUDIENCE(S)

As a first step you should go through the exercise of defining your audience(s). Many marketing experts call this process building your ideal buyers' *personas*.

Now, I know this is not everyone's favorite exercise, but it is critically important. You may be tempted to skip this step, especially if you haven't created personas before. Don't. It's not nearly as hard or complicated a process as many people think. Besides, if you do skip this step, you risk spending time on the wrong topics and creating content that will not support your marketing goals.

What is a persona?

It's a profile of your actual customers – built around who they are, what their responsibilities and goals are, what they're trying to solve or accomplish and what their role is in the buying cycle. If you sell multiple products, you may have multiple personas for each of your product lines.

If you haven't built personas before, here are a few suggestions to get started:

- **Talk to your sales and customer service teams**. They interact with your customers more than just about anyone in the company and should be able to give you some good ideas regarding what their persona is based on the definition above. They can definitely provide you with a list of common topics and questions, as well as the things that your customers *don't* care about.

- **Talk to your customers.** I'm always pleasantly surprised at how forthcoming customers can be in sharing what's important to them as buyers and what they expect from their vendors.

- **Look at your Web traffic, sales leads and visitors who stop by at trade shows.** Can you infer any insights into the profile of those who are requesting information?

- **Research on the Internet.** This may or may not be appropriate, depending on your industry and niche.

The demographics you choose to profile will vary depending on your company's product or service. For example, if you're selling clothing, jewelry or hair care products, it may be important to know if your buyers are male or female and what age group they're in. If you're selling financial software for accounting departments, those kinds of demographics may not be important.

As you work through this, don't worry about perfection. There is no right or wrong answer. The main goal is to avoid being too general. Here is an example of that:

Question: Can you tell me a little about your customers?
Answer: We sell office equipment to small-business owners.

You need to be able to describe this buyer in greater detail in order to create content that is going to sway them. If you're not sure where to begin, consider the example questions provided by digital marketing expert Laura Hampton:

"If your business is business-to-business, or B2B, consider the following about your target audience:

- Industry or sector
- Business size
- Business location
- How long they've been trading
- Seniority of target customer
- Role of target customer
- How the target customer typically researches new products or services
- How time rich or time poor they are
- Do they interact more on a mobile or a desktop device
- Who are they trying to target
- What challenges are faced by their role/business size/location/industry
- What does your product/service do for them

If your business is business-to-consumer (B2C), you'll be considering similar things but swap out business related elements for things like life stage, where they live and so on."[4]

It is very possible that you'll have both B2B and B2C buyers. For example, a healthcare company and an office supplies store could easily include both types of customers. If this is the case, you'll need to develop personas for both to ensure that you're addressing each of these buyer categories.

Ultimately, you're making the best-educated assumptions you can based on the collective input from the sources listed above. It's a starting point. As your content marketing strategy is launched and you can begin to track activity, you should be able to continue to refine these personas.

STEP 2: CREATE A PERSONA GRID

Once you've come up with the personas that you're going to be providing content for, put them on a grid and use it on a regular basis to check that you're staying focused. Here's a great worksheet by Margaret Hagen to help you get started:

---

4   Laura Hampton, "Techniques to Create a More Customer-Focused Content Plan," www.smartinsights.com/content-management/content-marketing-planning/tools-for-content-marketing, May 28, 2015.

Personas & Use Cases for Your Project's Three Main User Types				
USER 1:	Notes on them, preferences, frustrations, personality	How will they find your product?	What will their motivations be to use it?	How will they use it, step by step?
USER 2:	Notes on them, preferences, frustrations, personality	How will they find your product?	What will their motivations be to use it?	How will they use it, step by step?
USER 3:	Notes on them, preferences, frustrations, personality	How will they find your product?	What will their motivations be to use it?	How will they use it, step by step?

Source: Margaret Hagan, Personas and Use Case, Know Your Users Design Tool.

How you format the final results once you've created your personas of a typical buyer is up to you. I like to keep these simple, such as the following example from www.precisionmarketing.com:

Example Buyer Personas		
Buyer Name	**Purchasing Considerations**	**Decision Criteria**
Engineer	• Technical guidance • Innovative solutions • Product specifications • Updates on industry trends	• Instant information access • Accessible design help • Specific application solutions
Production Manager	• Ability to keep manufacturing lines optimized • Tight shipping deadlines • Connection with a live person for answers to a problem	• Service from a trusted source • Quality products • Fast delivery
Buyer	• Consensus between purchasing and engineering • Superior pricing • Strong relationships	• Competitive value • Superior value • Solid vendor partnership

Source: https://www.precisionmarketinggroup.com/blog/how-to-build-buyer-personas-for-an-industrial-marketing-plan

The following chart is yet another example with slightly different information. As you can see, the persona should be modified to include the key characteristics that help you identify the way your customers do their research and make buying decisions.

Facility/Operations Manager Fred	
	Company Information: • Industry: Distribution, manufacturing, 3PL • Yearly revenue: $20 million • Employees: 100
Personal Background: • Age: 45-55 • Married with one kid in college and one in high school • Education: undergraduate	**Goals and Challenges** • Success means: a raise and promotion • Values most: Job security, family, recognition for success, church • Biggest challenges: New systems, managing people, keeping all balls in air • Biggest objections: Appearance, liability, suitability, not state-of-the-art, look dumb
Role: Facility or Operations Manager • Job measured: space and operations efficiency, employee productivity • Skills required: people management, analysis, industry knowledge • Reports to CEO or general manager • Manages operations staff	**Shopping and Industry News Preferences** • Preferred communication: Email, phone • Use Internet for buying research: Much • Gets updated industry news: Specific industry publication • Industry publications: Trade magazines • Industry associations: Industry trade groups • Social network sites: LinkedIn?

Source: https://blog.bufferapp.com/marketing-personas-beginners-guide

I like the above two examples for keeping my buyer's challenges and values in mind. It's a great way to ensure that the final content is on point in addressing his or her buying process, challenges and values.

Again, there are no right or wrong ways to create persona charts. Search the phrase "persona grid" on the Internet and you'll quickly find many examples ranging from very simple to very detailed, such as the following chart:

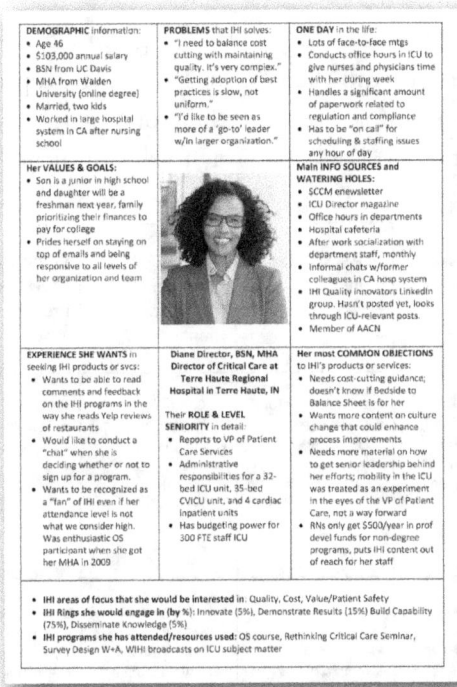

Source: https://blog.bufferapp.com/marketing-personas-beginners-guide

Any of these persona charts may work, depending on the product/service for which you are developing content. The key is to find one that works well for you.

STEP 3: DEVELOP A CONTENT GRID

After you've fleshed out your audiences and their personas, you can start developing a simple road map of how you're going to use your content to reach these audiences. I've seen many different road maps. Here are a few to give you some ideas.

The first example lists story ideas (blog, article, newsletter, etc.) in the left column and the personas across the top row. The grid is filled with examples of how the story may be messaged and conveyed in the most effective way to that audience.

Impression	PERSONA 1: Sally the Business Owner	PERSONA 2: James the Marketing Manager	PERSONA 3: Chris the Procurement Manager
STORY 1: Reputation and Long Established	• Company history • Client logos • Owner bio • Company's house info	• Company backstory • Time lapse video of business growth • Articles comparing then & now	• Client reviews • Case studies
STORY 2: Expertise of Team	• Blog posts from team members • Team qualifications • Business accreditations	• Industry-specific opinion articles • How to guides • Downloadable tools	• Data sheets • Product comparisons • Product applications how product can be used
STORY 3: Quality of Service or Product	• Client case studies • Videos of product manufacturing • Data sheets to compare services	• Client case studies • Product videos • Infographics to show complex service offerings	• Guarantees • Testimonials • Industry accreditations • Downloadable resources

Source: http://www.smartinsights.com/content-management/
content-marketing-planning/tools-for-content-marketing

The next example shows another way to group your communications according to each segment of personas you've defined.

If your customer is asking:	What is my problem?	How do I fix my problem?	Are you right for me?
Funnel stage:	Top of Funnel: Attract	Middle of Funnel: Nurture	Funnel Bottom: Sell
They want:	Education & Benchmarks	Solution Options & Product Sustainability	Proof Points & Decision Support
What to share with them:	• Trends • Benchmarks • Analyst coverage • 101 education • "How to" guides • How others are solving the problem	• What is the solution & how does it work • Solution comparisons • Pitfall analysis • Readiness & suitability assessments • How to choose a vendor	• Pricing • Bench strength demonstration • Case studies • ROI/TCO • Working with us • How to buy

Source: Nolin LeChasseur, Brainrider. http://www.legalsupportnetwork.
co.uk/marketing/resources/content-marketing-craze

The following chart by Go Lean Six Sigma may help you get started:

Communication Plan			
Stakeholder	Message	Delivery Method/ Venue	Timing

Source: Go Lean Six Sigma

Don't worry about completing an entire grid before you start your content marketing plans. If you haven't gone through this process or it's been sitting on the shelf, start with one or two personas and focus on them first.

Also, keep in mind that this isn't a one-time process. Buyers' preferences in how they want to be reached change as fast as new technology enters the market. Who could predict, for example, how quickly Pinterest or Instagram would become so important to consumers looking for ideas and products to buy? Once these platforms started catching shoppers' attention, many companies had to move quickly to adapt their sales channels accordingly.

That's why it's important to revisit your content marketing plan and be ready to adapt quickly.

For this reason alone, it's a good idea to put a note on your calendar to visit your communication plan and revise your grid on at least a monthly basis.

STEP 4: DO A CONTENT AUDIT

Before you even begin to think about what needs to be written, take the time to perform a content audit. This is one of the most effective, yet overlooked steps in the content generation process. It's easy to get caught up in thinking you need fresh content to get started, but in reality, you probably have some useful material in your existing marketing collateral.

As a first step, gather all of your company's existing marketing materials and create a library. This can include online and print materials new and old, such as:

- Sales literature
- Annual reports
- Press releases
- Previous newsletters and blog posts
- Guest articles
- Magazine articles about your company
- Old interviews
- Videos of product demos/discussions

- Case studies
- Reference materials
- Advertising campaigns

When I do this, I:

- Print everything out and lay it out on a table.
- Move the documents into groups as I skim them and categorize them.
- Jot down keywords to identify what the material is about in the margins.
- Highlight quotes or sections that look like they could be useful for other articles, blogs, etc.

Your first pass should be to identify what topics you have materials for. The next step is to identify which pieces have content that can be updated and reused. In many instances, you can revise content fairly easily and in a much shorter time period than it would take to create it from scratch.

Following are some examples of existing content that may just need a refresh:

- **Case studies**. If you find existing case studies that showcase a problem/solution scenario and are old but not obsolete, you can resurrect them by removing any specific customer names. If necessary, you can replace the company's actual name with a descriptive generic name. Instead of using "Abbott Insurance," replace it with "One of the world's largest insurers." If the case study is a few years old, remove the dates.

You may also find a case study with great customer quotes by a person who is no longer there. You can still use it by replacing the person's name with something like "Operations VP, Large Insurance Company." Another way to refresh a case study is to conduct a short interview with the customer and revise it accordingly.

- **Company articles**. Company-authored articles, even if they're old, are worth discussing. A product manager may say, "This is old news, we've advanced our product since this was published." Ask the manager what has changed and why. Product managers can typically concisely describe what is obsolete and what's new and better. You can use their comments as a starting point for an updated article.

- **Blog posts.** Blog posts are a great source of content that can be used in the "right now" and gathered for a larger project. (Note: We'll be discussing how to create blog posts later in the book.) Look over a series of older posts and see what can be repurposed. Is there a common theme that can be used to create a white paper or e-book?

For example, one company I worked with had launched a series of weekly blog how-to posts over a period of weeks to help manufacturers identify fulfillment processes that were resulting in higher shipping costs. We combined this collection of posts, added an introduction and summary, and turned it into a white paper for a successful email campaign. This same white paper also became the basis for an article in industry trade magazines.

- **Newsletter.** Newsletters, both online and/or older print versions, often contain very good information that is still very useful but has been forgotten. For example, one newsletter I worked on had a recurring "Frequently Asked Questions," or FAQ section that focused on product usage tips.

  Although the company's product had been upgraded since these newsletters came out, some of these FAQs still applied. We pulled out the useable content, updated it and launched a new online FAQ section on the company's new website.

- **Corporate videos.** A video that looks outdated can still be useful. In some cases, you can work with a video editor to revise and reuse it. Video scripts also can be mined for content. Customer quotes or testimonials in the video can be converted to short text quotes and included in other materials, provided they are officially approved by the customer and you don't change them.

- **Product demo videos**. These often contain the most concise descriptions of product features and benefits – even more so than written text sheets. I always watch them for this purpose. If the concept and script are really good but obsolete, they can serve as the framework to more quickly write a new script and produce a revised video.

- **Slide shows.** I'm always surprised by how much good material gets packed into presentations for specific events such as annual meetings, user conferences, trade shows, sales presentations, employee meetings, etc. Once the event is over, they get put on a shelf and forgotten, even though they're usually full of great content and visuals. It's worth skimming through them.

- **Media interviews.** Even if some of these interviews are old, you may be able to take sections of them and publish them on your website, newsletter or blog. If your CEO is talking about the company's mission or vision of the industry, for example, this may be timeless enough to reuse, particularly if you haven't shared it beyond a narrow audience.

These are just a few suggestions of ways to take a fresh eye to existing marketing materials. Look at everything you can get your hands on and ask questions about it all. Find out who contributed to the originals and, if you can, talk to them too. Ask them for ideas or stories of past campaigns that worked well. Many times, these conversations can result in unexpected ideas and hidden resources.

ASSESS THE VOICE OF YOUR EXISTING MATERIALS

While you're doing the audit, keep in mind that the content you find may be useable but the voice it's written in needs to be evaluated for appropriateness for your audience. Knowing their consumption preferences is critical to content marketing success.

Most companies are generating content for multiple audiences and it's good to keep that in mind as you're starting to audit what you have. As you begin to plan your content library, go back to your audience personas and jot down some of the characteristics of each of these readers. Keep these characteristics in front of you and do a reality check to make sure you're staying on track and addressing their points of interest in everything you produce.

That extra minute you take to do or not do this reality check is often the turning point at which you can win them or completely lose them. They have the luxury of choosing whether they want to continue to read after the first sentence or move on to something or someone else's content.

ESTABLISH THE RIGHT VOICE

Personas should help you define what you're going to actually talk about with each audience, but they should also influence the voice in which you write. In addition to providing the interesting and well-targeted information, you also need to present it in the way the reader is most likely expecting it.

In other words, there are times to be *selling* and times to be *educating*. If you mix them up, you can turn off your reader.

Following are some examples with a few tips to get you started:

- **Sales tools**. When writing product brochures, commercials, infomercials, etc., it's perfectly fine to call out your company's or solution's strengths and promote your brand. But it's critical to have a profile of the buyers in mind as you write this material. Take the time to ask your sales team and product managers questions to understand the typical buyer's function, pain points and value drivers.

  If you're selling project management software to a company, for example, you may find that management wants to know how it reduces labor and accelerates product development time-to-market, while actual project managers want to know if it's easy to use, helps them do their daily tasks and generates the tracking reports they need more easily.

- **Editorial content**. Let's say you're asked to take content from some of your promotional materials and turn it into an educational article for a trade journal. Before you start revising, take a little time to read previous issues of the journal to get a sense of the reader's education level. You can find out more about the reader profile in the magazine's media kit or by asking one of the editors.

  Generally the best approach is to avoid "selling" or overtly promoting the company. Take materials you have, strip that out, and put them back together as a best practices guide, how-to article, or future trends article. You get the idea.

- **Press/Media**. It's still true – editors tend to skip over press releases that are blatantly self-promotional and lack the facts. They're looking for the what, when, where, why in the release. For tips on how to shape an effective press release, please visit Chapter 7.

- **Social media**. What you post on LinkedIn is not necessarily the same content you'd post on Facebook, Twitter, Instagram. For one thing, each of these social media streams has its own length requirements, and the audiences come to them with different expectations. Image specifications are also different for each channel. If you're not sure of the differences between these channels, do some research on the Internet and/or engage a social media expert to ensure that you're posting in the most effective manner to drive results.

- **Newsletter**. Your newsletter can be composed of a blend of promotional and informational topics. In fact, I think you can actually build more credibility and rapport with your audience by including a mix of informational topics as well as how-to tips. Newsletters filled with promotional copy quickly become boring to readers and can result in higher unsubscribe rates. For more information about writing newsletters, refer to Chapter 8.

- **Blog**. Some companies may choose to use their blog as a promotional channel, while others use it as a means to build credibility by showing their industry expertise. If your blog is intended to be educational, that's how your posts should be focused. There are subtle ways to build your brand without being blatantly promotional. For example, you may include a sentence about your company in the closing paragraph, with a "contact us" for more information on the topic.

Also, don't create an educational title only to follow it with a sales pitch about why your solution is better. Readers are smart and impatient and will quickly abandon blog sites if they're misleading, so be clear in what you're presenting. That's the best tactic to build the audience you want.

- **Website content**. This is an entire topic unto itself. Suffice to say that your website is the place where you're probably serving the most audiences. It pays to take time to line up your audience list with your website pages and see if you're meeting their needs. You may even want to engage a content marketing specialist to help you audit your site and create a game plan.

STEP 5: SET PRIORITIES

Once you've completed the first two steps of creating personas and completing a content audit, you should have a good idea about where to begin in developing your content generation game plan. Chances are you've uncovered some materials that can be repurposed and you've identified gaps that need to be filled with new content.

The "where to begin?" question may be overwhelming, but you can put it to rest by creating a list that summarizes what you have and what you need. At this point, the most important step you can take is to allocate time that can be dedicated to getting your content writing plan moving. What if your audit reveals that you have nothing? The next chapter helps you get started with practical writing tips.

Two

Decide What to Write About

"Marketing used to be about making a myth and telling it. Now it's about telling a truth and sharing it."

— Marc Mathieu

If you're in the position of having very little content to start with, you're not alone. Many of my clients have relied on a handful of product brochures and a small website for years. You can ramp up fairly quickly by creating content generation project tracks that can be worked on simultaneously.

A MULTITRACK PLAN TO GET STARTED

Here are five content writing projects you can manage in parallel:

1. Company Products/Services
2. Case Studies
3. Blog Posts

4. Monthly Newsletter
5. Press Releases

I keep a monthly calendar in front of me and stagger the activities required for each of these projects so that they don't all occur on a certain day or in a certain week of the month.

TRACK 1: COMPANY PRODUCTS AND SERVICES

A bit of friendly advice: Just because your company has sales or product literature on hand, don't assume that these existing materials represent the most accurate or complete picture of your company's offerings.

As a starting point, ask your company's key stakeholders these simple questions:

- What do we sell?
- What benefit does it deliver?
- Who buys it?

This exercise could take minutes or hours. It's also easy to assume that everyone will come up with the same answers, but that's sometimes far from the case. It's always good to do a double-check to determine what's actually been written about each product/service.

If you sell multiple products and services, do you have content for each? You'd be surprised how often certain products are underrepresented in the marketing mix. Key information may have been written but got buried under other content, or it may not have been shared in any depth with the marketplace.

Do you know what priority is placed on each of your products/services in terms of driving revenue? This may not always be obvious at a first glance, especially if your company built its business on one product and then added to its product line over time.

For example, I worked with one company that started as a computer hardware reseller. As the market matured, the company added software products and technical services to its product line to differentiate itself from its competitors.

These new products and services were critical to the company's growth, yet they were hard to find on in the company's website and marketing campaigns. The company's message was still heavily "hardware" focused. Its website was made up of 90% hardware pages and 10% software pages.

When buyers went to the company website to learn more about its software solutions, they found a few pages that provided summary information. Consequently, the company was having a hard time building market awareness for its software.

This sounds like an extreme case of undermarketing, but this dilemma is more common than you'd think. If you find this to be true of your company, then:

- Create a product/solution grid,
- Prioritize the products according to their importance in the company's content strategy, and
- Fill in the gaps by writing the overview of the products that are missing.

In this case, we're not talking about purpose-driven content, just the overview. Once that is done, it can be edited and repurposed for many uses.

TRACK 2: REFRESH OR DEVELOP NEW CASE STUDIES

While you're working on product content, you can start building your case study library. Case studies are stories or vignettes that outline a particular company's challenge or problem and show how it solved the problem with your company's solution.

You can begin working on case studies in parallel with your other content writing projects because they don't always follow a step-by-step process that must be done in sequence. The process is much more fluid than that. It involves getting feedback from other team members, identifying client candidates and setting up interviews – a series of short interactions that take place over a period of days or weeks.

One place to start is to revisit the older case studies you identified in your content audit and figure out who on your team has the relationship with these customers. You may be able to refresh the content after an update from the account manager or by checking in with the customer for an update.

I once worked with a company that had shelved at least ten case studies because they were old. Unfortunately, they didn't have the resources to cultivate new ones, so they had no case studies for their website or their sales kits. We solved the problem by taking a two-pronged approach:

- We edited the old case studies and repackaged them with new headlines and a fresh layout. In some cases, we were able to speak with the customer and add new elements to the story.

- At the same time, we worked with the sales and support team to build a list of at least ten additional customers and invited them to participate in our case study program.

You may ask, "why so many?" because rarely do they progress in a predictable manner or pace. I've found it works best to keep a series of case study opportunities in the queue because these projects are dependent upon customers' timelines and priorities and they take extra time to schedule and complete.

Even if you only have one or two case studies to begin with, you can use them very effectively by packaging them in multiple ways. For example, you can:

- Create a complete pdf that can be used by the sales team or downloaded by visitors to your website.
- Extract the customer quotes as stand-alone testimonials on your website, in presentations and in other materials.

- Create a synopsis of the story and use it as a pitch to editors.
- Create a slideshow that visually tells the story.

For tips about writing case studies, refer to Chapter 5.

TRACK 3: CREATE BLOG POSTS

Creating a blog can be a very effective way to keep your company and brand in front of prospects and customers without offending them by constantly selling. However, in order to be effective, your blog posts have to be educational in tone and content and offer useful advice, knowledge or answers to questions for the reader. They cannot be thinly veiled promotional posts or they will have the opposite effect – driving your reader away.

If you're just getting started with a blog, it can be daunting to come up with topics. One way to start is to take the same group of keywords or concepts that you've identified for your search engine optimization (SEO) campaigns and develop content based on these same topics.

ORIGINAL CONTENT OR RESHARES?

When you're faced with the task of posting on a regular basis and pressed for time, it can be tempting to simply reshare other people's posts. This may solve your frequency problem but will not be as effective in generating interest. In my experience, original content, if it is useful and well written, drives much higher reader loyalty than posts that are simply reshares of other content. When I've compared reader traffic based on original versus reposted content, the numbers have been very telling.

This is not to say I don't use other content. But when I do, I make sure to create an original post with freshly written original paragraphs. If I am going to showcase someone else's content, I may write a few lead-in paragraphs and then introduce the article and provide the link, such as in the example below. I also make sure it includes my audience's keywords and topics.

In other cases, I will write an original blog post that covers a topic that may have been written about in the past by several other publications. In this case, I take a fresh angle on it, and if I use any of the material from other articles or posts, I make sure to credit the author, such as in the example below.

I'm always working on blog posts in parallel with all other marketing campaigns, and the schedule includes a range of topics that may be featured in the company newsletter, and on social media sites such as LinkedIn, Facebook, Google+ and Twitter. Note that you may have to create a slightly different lead-in for the blog post on each of these sites.

TRACK 4: SEND A NEWSLETTER

If you're already working on content such as blog posts, press releases and product notes, you can repurpose all of these content pieces in your future newsletters and save a tremendous amount of time in creating each issue.

The best way to flesh out your newsletter planning schedule is to use your overall content calendar. If you do a quick search on the Web, you'll find many different examples of calendars and software tools to help you manage.

TRACK 5: WRITE PRESS RELEASES

Many companies are very good at keeping a steady stream of press releases in the queue to announce awards won by the company, new products, new offices, recent hires, speaking engagements, new partnerships or professional affiliations, philanthropy, etc. Just as many fail to take advantage of this publicity channel.

Press releases, when released through press release (PR) distribution outlets and posted on your website, are not only very effective in building awareness, but they're an important signal to Google that you're creating fresh content. They can also be used in your newsletter, sales kits, media kits, etc.

To get started, read Chapter 7.

FIND GOOD SOURCES

As you're thinking about keeping all these project tracks in play, you're probably also wondering how you can possibly get enough content to keep it going. This is an aspect of content writing that I once worried a lot about – trying to figure out who could help me figure out what to say about a topic I was not an expert on.

Whether you're the marketer, the product manager, or even the writer, you're not alone. There are multiple sources around you that can help you, but you have to proactively seek input and ideas. As writer Jack London said, "You can't wait for inspiration. You have to go after it with a club."

Here are some of the sources I use:

EMPLOYEES

Whether you're working as a consultant or are an employee of the company, you'll find that employees are a gold mine. Depending on the size of the organization, you may begin by talking to the product managers, sales team, customer service team, and senior managers who may have been involved with the development of its product or service.

These people can help you very quickly narrow down the list of what to write about, so that you don't have to spend long hours searching on the Internet or through reference materials to try and determine the content priorities.

For example, I was working with a company that sold a line of software solutions as well as mobile computers, scanners and printers. At first glance at the company's product line, I was not sure where to begin in determining which products were the most important to write about.

A quick interview with one of the senior salespeople helped me understand how the software products worked with each other and which were the biggest sales drivers. He could also tell me the key questions prospects were asking when he made sales calls.

I next wanted to understand how the software and hardware products fit together in a sales call. A quick interview with another senior salesperson who focused more on the hardware side answered those questions for me, and an interview with the founder helped me understand how the company differentiated itself by selling both product lines.

PROFESSIONAL PEERS

Ask your co-workers if they can introduce you to other professional peers who would be good candidates for an interview.

For example, many times, if I'm talking to a salesperson about what she thinks we should be writing about, she will share her hot topics and can often come up with industry professionals who would also be a good source. They may be a customer, or a company that offers a complementary solution so they're in the same market but are not competitors.

EDITORIAL AND INDUSTRY CONTACTS

I also contact editors or marketing directors for industry associations in pursuit of resources. These people are often very willing to point you in the direction of potential contacts and sources. They themselves are often willing to talk because it is in their own professional interest to network with you.

Once I make contact with editors, there are those who you'll build a natural rapport with, especially if you've been providing them with good non-promotional content such as educational articles, case studies, etc. I often ask these peers when I am trying to get a pulse on what's trending among readers.

CUSTOMERS

Your customers are also a great source of good topics for content marketing. I usually work through a salesperson or someone in the company who keeps a pulse on customer relationships and can make an introduction for me to someone who is willing to share ideas. I ask them, "What does someone in your position spend his time thinking about in order to achieve your company's goals?" What follows is almost always quite illuminating. So many people put so much time and effort into their work and their company that they're delighted when someone shows a genuine interest.

OTHER SOURCES FOR TOPICS

Sometimes I work with clients who do not have time to come up with ideas and want me to come up with them. If they're industry topics I'm familiar with, I know where to look and who to talk to in fairly short order.

But sometimes they send entirely new topics my way and I need a quick start to figure out what is trending. If I don't have someone to ask, I look to other resources for ideas, such as the agendas of online webinars or conferences, online publications, books, articles and posts.

YouTube can also be a source. There are multitudes of videos showcasing panels of experts speaking on a topic. In this as in any channel, be sure you verify the source for credibility.

NARROW THE TOPIC LIST

At first, you may find that you're getting a smattering of suggestions that cover a wide range of topics, but after a few conversations with people who are in the know on that industry topic, you'll start to see some topics emerge more repetitively than others. You'll probably also get some ideas for new topics that haven't really been covered well at that point.

In general, I ask enough people so that common topics become clear to me. I then back it up by searching the same topics on the Internet.

BUILD AN IDEA GENERATOR

If you're responsible for generating content on an ongoing basis, you're going to need to build your own resource library as a means to help you work efficiently. This is that collection of interesting articles, websites, posts and notes from conversations that you encounter as part of your day-to-day routine.

I often stumble across new story ideas while I'm in the process of researching a specific topic. I don't want to get sidetracked from the work at hand, but don't want to forget the idea, so I've come up with a way to hang on to interesting materials for a later date.

The key to making all the background tidbits you're finding useful is to keep them organized so that you don't have to spend more time searching piles of documents for that one specific piece of information you know you saved, but can't remember exactly where.

BUILD AN IDEA LIBRARY

I'll say right now that there is no one way to build a useful and convenient library. Everyone has his or her own way of collecting useful information. My friend David, for example, prefers to store everything online. My sister uses Pinterest. Others may choose to print everything they find. I use both print and electronic cataloging methods. When I'm in the process of researching online, I use the bookmark feature on the Web browser to tag articles that I want to read later. I also use OneNote.

I also have a file cabinet where I store print versions by topic so that I can easily grab whatever I've amassed, spread it out on a table and see how much I have to start on a project. Usually, I have written notes on the top and margin of the documents, which helps me instantly recall why I thought it was useful without having to read the entire piece again.

Whether you prefer online or printed versions, I'd recommend you make folders for the general topics you think you'll be writing about and start moving all those documents you've saved into them. Over time, you'll notice that certain folders don't seem to get much added to them at all, while you seem to have plenty to add to others.

You may also find that you have this miscellaneous pile of background material that you find interesting, but don't have a folder for it. These things give you clues as to how to modify your library and make it more efficient.

Allow yourself the luxury of collecting a wider range of background materials than you need for the project at hand. You won't use it all right away, but keep building for the future. I've found that while my conscious brain is focused on a specific topic, my subconscious is also at work, pulling together other great ideas. The cool thing is that I'm not even aware it's happening until it's over. Later on in that day, new ideas will come to me that were the direct result of that targeted work.

INTERVIEW AS A MAINSTAY

Hands down, one of the most useful ways to spend time researching is to interview someone who has direct experience, knowledge or ideas in the area you're building content. This is critical for several reasons.

They can save you immense amounts of time narrowing your list of topics to the most important for your project objective. They can also help you prioritize topics and sources in terms of their importance. The key is to make sure you're interviewing the right person for the objective you have in mind. For example, let's say you're given the mandate to build a content strategy that builds awareness for your company's expertise in designing and building eco-friendly living spaces.

- Interviews can help you by ensuring that you're using the industry terminology and/or jargon in the correct way.

- They can help you get a better understanding of what's on the minds of your company/client's customers/ partners/associates.

- They can help you understand where your company's value lies, where you stand in terms of the market and your competitors, etc.

- They can point you in the direction of pertinent sources for good background information.

- They can line up introductions for interviews with customers, subject-matter experts, and industry spokespeople.

If you tried to accomplish all of these things on your own, it would take an inordinate amount of time. A 30- or 60-minute interview can help you quickly determine where you need to be focused.

There is one other aspect of interviewing that I've found to be extremely helpful. If I am talking to pioneers in an industry or entrepreneurs, I find they are more than willing to share their ideas on other topics. For example, I might ask them what they think the world will look like in ten years, what they attribute their own success to, and what they're concerned about today. Many times, these informal conversations have yielded new interviews and new stories.

For example, I once interviewed a consultant who was a well-respected expert on the topic of mergers and acquisitions (M&A). I asked him how to conduct effective due diligence on a company being considered for potential acquisition. He covered this topic thoroughly but the more we talked, it became clear that his specialty was working with distressed companies, not healthy companies.

We got to talking about what it took for an M&A professional to actually know what to do in a distressed situation. At this point, we came up with another story – which was about what it takes to be successful in the M&A world of distressed companies. We ultimately wrote two additional sections to the book, featuring him as well as several other "distressed" investors.

This is just one example of many instances where interviews have yielded additional topics and opened the door to an ongoing relationship with a great professional resource.

Three

Writing Tips

*"If you think you have writer's block,
lower your expectations."*

— Sandra Tsing Loh

The content audit, research and/or interviewing is done. Now it's time to do the writing. This will probably include a combination of projects in which you're editing existing materials that you discovered in your audit and writing entirely new content to fill in the gaps you identified.

If you find yourself in the role of writer, even though you've never intended to be one, this chapter is for you. It's safe to say I've met far more people who dread or dislike writing than those who enjoy it. I've worked with clients who are hesitant to write because it's been such a very long time since they had to write that they are uncertain where or how to begin.

I've also worked with many clients who have product or industry knowledge, but never really had to write about it before. Someone else usually handled it, but now it's part of their job. It's not surprising that the writing falls to the bottom of their to-do list. Who'd want to do what they're not trained to do?

I'm convinced that most people dread writing projects because they have a preconceived notion that they're writing for a Pulitzer. Relax. That's not the goal here. Content generation is about providing information, not writing for theater. The good news is that you will, I believe, find the writing process to be much easier to manage if you keep a few things in mind. The following tips, I have found, get you to a finished product faster, with less edits and angst.

WRITE LIKE YOU SPEAK

One of the main reasons that people are intimidated by writing is the common perception that they need to assume a different voice. This is especially true if your writing experience is largely based in writing scholarly essays or compositions.

Content writing isn't about that. Most of the time, what you're writing is going to be explanatory and maybe promotional. The best place to start is to write like you speak – at work, that is. In this case, write like you speak about your company, your products, or your services.

FIND YOUR VOICE

So go ahead. Grab a cup of coffee and think of a topic that you're naturally interested in. It doesn't have to be about work, since this is just an exercise to start getting comfortable with writing. I might, for example, choose to write about what makes for a perfect cup of coffee because I love it, have spent a fair amount of time studying it and am familiar with the subject matter. Or you can choose a product/topic that is work-related. That works fine too.

Next, think about what you say when you're talking about this subject to your peers. Now just start writing. Don't worry about fixing your grammar or choosing better words as you go. Just keep writing about the topic. Don't edit. Just write until you can't write anymore – ideally a page or a few pages.

Now look through what you wrote. Chances are good that your writing started out a little formal and maybe even a little "stiff," but it loosened up as you kept writing. If you give it a chance, you'll find that this is common. What happens is that your sub-liminal brain actually kicks in and starts writing for you.

Do this a few times and I will bet that your real voice starts to emerge, in a more natural cadence, and the words themselves become more concise too, because as you let go of the process and let your brain do the writing, it naturally finds its way.

Someone once described the brain to me as a muscle that needs to be worked on a regular basis, just as you'd work your other muscles if you want to keep them in top form. It's true. Writing is also very much like a muscle. If you tap into that part of your brain that you use to write, on a regular basis, it responds more readily and the writing flows more freely.

Especially when you stop thinking you have to write like Einstein or Hemingway.

START WITH AN OUTLINE

Here's another tip that is worth its weight in gold. Always start with an outline, no matter how rudimentary. Doing so makes your brain go through the exercise of formulating the concept and jotting down the framework of your piece. I've written them on the back of a product brochure, a cocktail napkin, even on the back of my electricity bill envelope. They all worked just fine and I referred to them as I fleshed out the draft.

It doesn't need to be pretty or polished. It's the act of framing your idea and referring back to that simple outline that keeps you on track and prevents you from writing entire sections that don't belong.

Do I write without an outline? Some people do, and reorganize after they've created a draft. I don't, because after assessing projects that were harder to complete than others, I realized that most often when I've been stuck, it's because I didn't have an outline or forgot to look at it.

APPROACH THE WRITING IN STAGES

Some people can sit down and complete a writing project in one session, start to finish. In reality, that's the exception rather than the rule. If you think that's the way it's supposed to be done, you're setting yourself up for stress.

The most efficient and effective approach, for me, is to take the writing process in stages:

1. Establish the thesis.
2. Gather background information.
3. Organize it into an outline.
4. Flesh it out into a draft.

Depending on the length and scope of a project, these stages may go very quickly or involve more writing, but I don't skip these steps.

For example, if you're writing a short blog on a narrowly defined topic or a press release, you'll probably be able to move through these stages fairly quickly.

If you're working on a bigger project, such as a white paper focused on emerging business trends and how companies are adapting, the process may take longer.

The key is to allow yourself enough time. Press releases and blog posts can be written in hours, so it's possible that you'll go through these steps and create a good final document "same day."

Needless to say, don't wait until the last minute to write an entire article or white paper. That leads to stress, poor product and missed deadlines. Plan ahead and give yourself enough time, and the writing is much easier to manage.

ESTABLISH THE THESIS AND GOAL

Thesis is a big word for goal, in my opinion. Don't let the word make you think you're writing a dreaded essay. Think of it as the underlying reason behind whatever you're writing. Whenever I begin a project, I make sure to ask these questions:

- What is the intention behind writing this?
- Who is the audience?
- What is the underlying premise of the article? What is more important to include?
- What do we want the reader to do with the information?

Whether you're working with co-workers such as product managers or a sales/marketing team, or you're being hired by a company to do the writing, it's always good to go over those questions with the client.

You'd be surprised how often the project "owner" hasn't had the time to think these aspects of the project all the way through, or how often the final piece will have multiple audiences and objectives. The best outcomes occur when expectations are clearly set at the beginning and clearly understood by the client.

NOTES WHILE I'M RESEARCHING

The subliminal part of the writing process begins, for me, when I am doing the background research for a writing project. At this point, I'm gathering my thoughts while I read so that I can summarize my findings later. If I'm writing an article about a company's product, I may be pulling other articles or existing materials from the company. I may be reading interview transcripts.

It works very well to print hard copies of whatever materials I'm reading and jot down short notes or callouts along the margins. Later, I collect all of these background pieces, lay them out on my worktable and start to organize them into logical groups. With the notes and callouts marked, I can quickly refer to key points that may go into the outline.

For articles, I write summary sentences, noting the key point that may be useful. For interviews, I read the written transcript and highlight those parts that I think will go into the final piece. It's important to note that this is the starting point where I'm shaping the general thesis and supporting points. I'll sort through the notes later and use them to shape my outline.

It's important to do your research in a directed, but objective manner.

A PROVEN STEP-BY-STEP WRITING PLAN FOR GREAT RESULTS

1.   FROM RESEARCH NOTES TO AN OUTLINE

This is the process I use when I'm not seized by inspiration that's so compelling I can jot my outline down on an envelope while I'm at the airport. Once I've gotten to the point that I believe I have enough background information to help me write the introduction, the middle and the end, I work up an outline. It's not usually too long or detailed. The intent is to start to formulate my thoughts into a logical flow. I may not have all the details, but that's all right. I put a placeholder in the outline for information I know I need to go back and find.

Reality Check: Who Is the Audience?

I mention this question again because it's so easy to forget this most important question as you progress through a project. While you're in the process of doing your research, talking to others who are weighing in on the project, it's easy to forget that all of the information you're gathering and advice you're getting needs to be viewed through a filter – the audience.

So just jot down who the audience members are, what their interests are and keep that at the top of the page so you can look back frequently. This helps when you find yourself getting sidetracked and can prevent you from wasting time writing about a lot of extra ideas that may be great, but don't fit into the piece.

Once I've completed the outline, I send it to my clients for a quick review, just to make sure I am on track with the direction of the piece and also to solicit any feedback that may help further develop it.

I should note that my outlines are not the traditional outlines we learned to write in school. Instead, I use an outline style that gives my client a sense of the direction of the paper, the voice, and an indication of quotes/references to be included.

2.   FROM OUTLINE TO DRAFT ONE

Once the outline is approved, I expand it into an actual draft of the piece. When writing this draft, I don't spend much time trying to come up with a great title and sizzling introduction. I just write a very basic title and include the basic facts/premise of the piece at this point.

I've found that I can waste immense amounts of time trying to get these things right early in the process. In reality, it's too early. I get the best results when I finish them last.

To get into the flow, I skip the title and introduction and start fleshing out the outline into a full narrative that expands on the bare-bones phrases in the outline. A two-page outline may expand into five pages. At this stage, I'm aiming for as close to final voice as I can. This is the draft I would show to my subject-matter experts or clients – after I've given it a rest and have had a chance to edit it.

At this point, I am once again looking for feedback to ensure that the piece is heading in the right direction or learn where/how I am off base. I also ask clients to identify any corrections relating to the content, omissions of important information, and general feedback. Based on these edits and comments, I finalize the piece.

3. EDIT THE DRAFT

As much as I have encouraged you to write that first draft without putting your editor cap on, I recommend that you allow enough time for a round of editing. It can be difficult to do if you're working under tight deadlines, but trust me, this is important.

There are times when I've worked under such tight deadlines that we had one day to go from start to finish in researching and writing a piece for public consumption, with no time for an editing round. Yes, we hit the deadline, but the writing, in my mind, was not as polished as it could have been. Even stepping away from it for an hour would have made a world of difference.

Let's assume you've completed your draft and had a day or so to let it rest. Now is the time to edit. Your goal is to improve the writing by making it cleaner. If you've had a chance to step away from the writing, you'll have a more objective eye and instinct about what needs to be done. At this stage I go through and ask myself:

- Did I write this with the audience's interest in mind? Does it wander away from that focus? Where?

- Is it written at the appropriate level of knowledge for the audience? I always try to ask someone who has a good understanding of the audience to review the piece with this in mind. If you're writing for multiple levels of comprehension, it can be tricky to determine what the best level is. If it's too elementary for your readers, you'll lose them. In this case, it's always good to have "Learn More" options for those readers who may be looking for more in-depth information.

- Does the piece convey the objectives that it is intended to? If it is to educate, does it do that? If it is to convince the reader to take an action, is that clearly laid out? If it is to build brand, does it do that?

- Another thing I step back and ask myself is, does it tell too much? For example, if I'm writing a blog post in which the goal is to get the reader to call the company for more information, does it stop at the right point in time or does it give the readers so much information that they don't feel compelled to call? This is a common mistake.

- These kinds of questions are about qualitative editing – something that you and your subject-matter experts can weigh in on. At this stage your written piece may undergo rewriting and reorganization. That's normal.

There is another kind of editing that should also take place – copy-editing. Copy-editing is the practice of reviewing the written piece for grammar, punctuation and spelling. At this point, the editing is limited to making sure the writing is correct – rather than reworking it for qualitative issues. If you don't have experience with copy-editing or are not strong in this area, it may be worthwhile to engage a copy editor's services.

If you are the writer and the final copy editor, allow some time to pass between drafting and finalizing.

TIPS TO IMPROVE YOUR PROCESS

Probably the most important premise of writing well is to avoid procrastination. I know it's hard not to put off working on a new writing project, especially if it's new subject matter or a project that you're not particularly wild about. As my mother would say, "Putting it off will only make you feel worse."

It's even difficult not to procrastinate when you're working on something you love. But hands down, waiting until the last possible minute to do the research and write the final piece is a sure way to guarantee that it won't be your best work.

If you're about to start a project you're dreading, or your workload is huge and you're not even sure how you're going to get the writing done, these tips may help.

- **Break it into smaller chunks of work and put them on your calendar.** I find this very helpful to get me moving on projects that seem daunting. For example, rather than saying I'm going to spend all day researching and then writing an outline, I instead block out an hour on my calendar dedicated to researching a topic.

- **Read in chunks.** I don't do a deep reading of each piece of material I find at that time; I just focus on gathering multiple sources that look like they have merit. I then schedule a separate hour or two at a time dedicated to reading – as many blocks of time as it takes to get it done.

This takes the pressure off feeling that I have to have a plan start to finish right from the get go, an unrealistic expectation when the work involves new territory.

The power of this approach is that it makes me feel less pressured, and while I'm poking around for sources, my subconscious is already starting to sort out the potential story line for me.

- **Allow time to step away and gain a fresh perspective.** This doesn't mean taking days or weeks away from the research or the writing. On the contrary, too much of a gap in time can cause you to lose momentum. Besides, most of the time, we don't have that luxury. Deadlines are always tighter than we wish.

What I am suggesting is to allow a day, a few hours or even 15-minute breaks from what you're working on. By this I mean taking the mental step of stepping away from the project and turning your mind to other tasks or activities.

I've found this to be one of the most valuable tips out there to keep me on task, prevent me from going too far off on tangents, and produce the best quality of work. It works well throughout the process. For example, I try to build in a day or a half day:

- After the outline is done.
- After the first draft is done.
- After I've finished the final draft – before I send it to the client or project manager.

If you can give yourself this amount of time off, you'll come back to the work with a sharp eye that makes it much easier to home in on aspects of the writing you didn't notice before, and you probably wouldn't notice if you just "plowed" on through to the finish.

EDIT WITH A FRESH EYE

Breaks are very productive. If I do take the time to step away, when I come back, I can usually spot things that will improve the content pretty quickly such as:

- **Improve the flow.** When you're writing a first draft, it's not always easy to see that your ideas and/or paragraphs don't flow in a logical path. This sticks out like a sore thumb if you've had a chance to step away and take a fresh look.

- **Tighten up the content.** By this I mean, noting areas where you may not have explained something as fully as is necessary and other areas where you've delved into too much detail. Sometimes I find myself writing very well on a certain topic, but when I step back, it's clear that although I may be enamored with that chunk of content, it doesn't really fit or isn't necessary. Stepping away helps you see this more quickly.

I also step away, even for 15 minutes, when writing isn't going well and I'm laboring too much or spending too much time on a certain section. When you're in the thick of it, it can be hard to stop writing, but if you get that feeling that you're reworking the same small group of words over and over and they're not getting any better, it's time to stop. Get a fresh cup of coffee, go for a short walk, just take a break. When you return to the work, you'll probably see another way to approach the writing that you're stuck in.

WRITE FIRST, EDIT LATER

This was one of the harder things to teach myself but it's truly the best way to write – and the fastest way to create a finished product. Once you have your outline finished and are going to write your piece, do just that and don't start editing until you've got that first draft down.

It's quite instinctive to want to stop and fix your writing when you're getting your thoughts down on paper. That temptation only grows when you've been writing for a while and are somewhat familiar with your own writing voice. I'm tempted to edit these paragraphs as I'm putting them together for the first time, but I know from experience that doing so at this stage is a trap.

First of all, editing while you're getting the first draft down on paper distracts you from the bigger objective of getting the "meat" of your story or article down. Instead, your mind goes into the micro-focus of picking just the right words, rearranging, shortening, etc. In other words, your mind shifts from creating content to editing for language and style. If you do this, you actually divert your brain from creative magic to tactical wordsmithing.

The way out of this trap is to stop yourself from going back to any sentence while you're in creation mode. Just keep writing. Tell yourself that you'll have plenty of time to go back over the draft later.

If you find yourself being a constant editor, even in your first draft, just once, try ignoring the edit impulse and writing "through" and editing later. I think you'll find that you actually get through to the finished piece more quickly by following this process. Not only that, the final piece you write probably has a better cadence and flow than if you'd allowed yourself to continue editing along the way.

DON'T WRITE IN A VACUUM

Here is another bit of wisdom that has helped me keep projects moving. It's very easy to squirrel yourself away and work alone as you do the research and start to shape your written piece. But sometimes, I've found that I actually make unnecessary work for myself when I do too much of the work in isolation.

For example, I was working on a white paper that was intended to educate the audience on best practices to eliminate costs in their operations and fulfillment areas. I assumed my readers were well versed in industrial automation and expected advanced discussion. Consequently, I assumed I had to write this paper at a college level for industrial engineers, which meant writing at a pretty sophisticated level of detail.

In reality, it wasn't what was called for at all.

Most of the readers were operations staff who may have had some level of industrial automation experience, but their company was still using manual processes to fulfill orders. The paper really needed to be an introduction to provide readers with a general overview of automation options and some basic factors to consider in assessing and adopting automation.

One way to avoid this misconception of the audience is to scope out the territory before you start. For example, it's a good idea to:

- **Download some industry magazines**. Check the level of the writing in them and read what others are writing in the same subject. If you're not sure which magazines to choose, ask your peers, sources and/or customers.

- **Ask peers before you start writing**. This may be, for example, salespeople and support people who routinely talk to customers of the profile you're writing about. They can tell you what common questions come up and what a "day in the life" of the audience looks like.

- **Validate industry-specific jargon by asking someone who works in that industry.** Phrases and buzzwords fall out of favor. It's always good to find out how people are describing their world before you start writing.

When I am trying too hard and getting nowhere, I also read "like" articles. This helps me realize where I need to focus my efforts.

Four

How to Write Blogs

"Blogs are the marketing 'equalizer' that I've searched for my entire career."

— Stan Smith

WHAT IS A BLOG?

By now, we've all read blogs of many forms, written for personal, educational and business consumption. People also have widely varying ideas of specifically what a blog is. To find out how diverse the answers can be, just search "definition of a blog" in Google.

Since we're focusing on generating content that builds your company's brand and converts prospects into customers, let's focus on a definition that fits this purpose. The Oxford Dictionary defines a blog as, "A regularly updated website or web page, typically one run by an individual or small group, that is written in an informal or conversational style."[5]

I think of a business blog as a place for the company to share value-added information that goes beyond traditional sales content. The first step to creating content is to determine your audience(s) and develop a list of topics that will be interesting to them.

For example, I was charged with developing a blog for a company that sells shipping software for online retailers. The audience was made up of owners, as well as operations and IT managers who are responsible for fulfillment operations. After some thought, the first topics we settled on for the blog site were:

- Trends in shipping costs and how to control them
- New technology solutions to speed operations and reduce labor costs
- Updates on their customers' buying patterns and service expectations
- Updates on how their competition was tackling the same issues
- Recommendations to help online retailers learn about shipping internationally

In writing these blogs, our goal was to provide readers with a good summary of the issue at hand, backed by industry surveys and examples from like companies, and provide other resources to help them become more informed. We cited the company as

---

5 www.oxforddictionaries.com/us/definition/american_english/blog

the author and thought leader in the technology space. The goal was to guide these readers to inquire at the company when they want to upgrade their systems. It's working very well.

The other aspect of developing the target audience for your blog is to know each member of your customer's buying team and keep these personas in front of you as your write your blogs. Building a persona is not the same as capturing demographics. Buyer personas are representations of your actual customers — taking into account who they are, what they are trying to accomplish, what their goals are, and how they behave throughout the buying cycle.[6] That is the surest way to write content that will get them engaged with your company. For more information on how to create personas, refer to Chapter 1.

HOW LONG SHOULD A BLOG POST BE?

There is no simple answer to this question. If you're writing for the human reader, the quality of the content, more than the length, should be the priority.

For years, the ideal blog length tossed about was 400 to 500 words. Long blogs of 1,500 to 2,000 words were not recommended, based on the premise that readers would lose interest. In reality, if you've done your homework on your personas and are providing really useful and interesting information in your blog, you'll keep your reader's attention.

---

6   Arnie Kuenn, "Why You Need a Persona-Based Content Marketing Strategy,"marketingland.com/why-you-need-persona-based-content-marketing-strategy-125582/, May 4, 2015.

Blogger Julie Neidlinger says it well: "People will read what is interesting and what they want to learn. It may happen to be 2,000 words, or it might be 800. Our attention span is never dead when it has to do with something we are truly curious about or that feeds our inner ego. Outside of that realm, people will skim and skip."[7]

Another content expert, Medium.com, has taken another approach to understanding what word length will yield the best reader results. According to its research, posts that take seven minutes to read are the ideal length. Here are the company's research results:

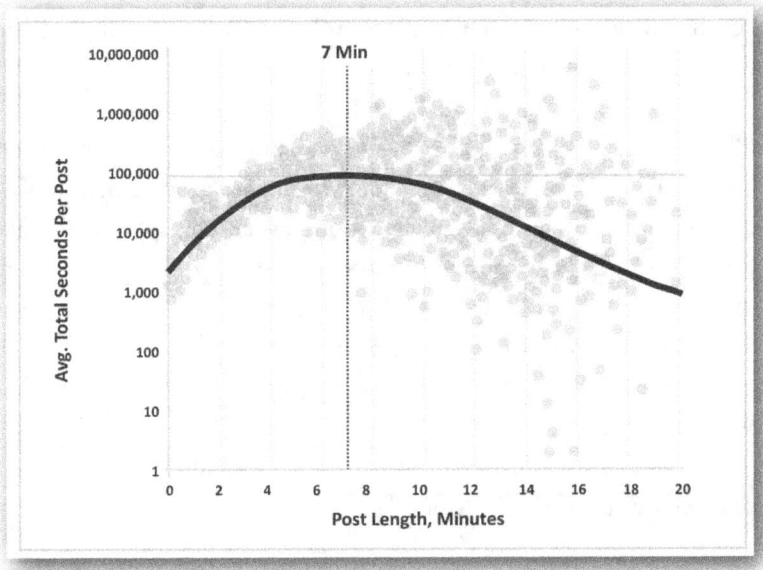

Source: Medium.com

---

7   Julie Neidlinger, "What Really Is the Best Blog Post Length?" coschedule.com/blog/blog-post-length/

A seven-minute read, according to Medium, translates into roughly a 1,700-word post, which is within the same realm of an ideal post for SEO ranking. Now, if you're an experienced writer, you know how much research and preparation goes into creating anything of that length. *A lot.*

However, before you get too concerned about having to ramp up to long-form posts, every day, keep in mind that this is an ideal to strive for, and it may not be a fit for all companies. Some bloggers such as Seth Godin, for example, are known for posting very short yet effective posts every day. Many of his blogs, I would venture to guess, are fewer than 200 words, but I still find the content to be immensely useful.

Dan Primack, senior editor of *Fortune*, publishes the *Term Sheet* every day, but varies the length of his posts. Sometimes he includes a fairly in-depth article about aspects of private equity deals or trends, and on other days he adds a running summary of deals taking place. Both work well, but I'd suspect that the in-depth articles take longer to write than the deal rolls. Either way, he is able to stay in front of his constituents with information that they deem useful.

DON'T LET WORD LIMITS AFFECT CONTENT QUALITY

I've worked on projects that had a fixed word limit of 400 to 500 words, regardless of the topic for the company's blog site. My job was to rework existing blogs that had been written by an internal party so that they were sufficiently different than the original and could be placed in another site. What I noticed in some of these blog posts was that the 400- to 500-word limit for the article was too short to really offer enough information to satisfy the reader.

Due to the detailed nature of the topics that were chosen, 400 to 500 words were simply not enough to build a compelling story. In this case, if the blog posts had been expanded to 1,000 words, they could have included that next level of information that readers would naturally be looking for. I've also worked on long blog posts of 1,000 to 2,500 words that proved to be very effective in attracting readers.

If your company already has a blog in place, you can do some informal research to get a better understanding of what your readers prefer. How much activity do your shorter blogs get versus your longer blogs? Is there a difference in reader engagement? Of course, there are other elements that affect reader engagement as well, such as the effectiveness of the blog's title. Good title, SEO optimized, with good content – you need it all.

WRITING BLOGS FOR GOOGLE SEARCH

Keep in mind, you're not just writing for humans, you're also writing to build your company's presence in Google Search. As many experts will tell you, Google seems to prefer longer content.

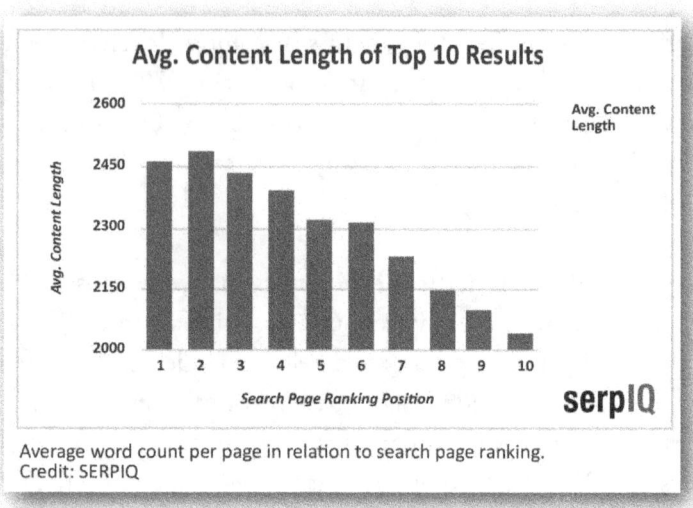

Average word count per page in relation to search page ranking.
Credit: SERPIQ

How does this work? A Forbes article by John Rampton summarized it well:

> According to some incredibly detailed research from serpIQ, the top 10 results from Google all have a minimum of at least 2,000. The reason? Because Googlebot, Google's web crawler, looks at every piece of content on a page, such as words, titles and whatever other information you've shared. So, when you have a post that has like 1,500 words you have more flexibility with keywords, meaning that you're not limited to one or two specific keywords. Instead, you can include a lot more of keywords that may not be specific, but are still relevant to your theme. This works because

Google just doesn't provide exact results, but results that are related to the subject.[8]

Notice that Rampton talks about keywords as an integral part of the blog-writing process. It's a good idea to map your post ideas to specific keywords and keep track of them to make sure they didn't get omitted from the final draft. For information on where to add keywords, refer to Chapter 11.

HOW OFTEN SHOULD YOU POST A NEW BLOG?

This answer will vary depending upon the kind of company you're writing for, the customer demographic and the availability of other resources to help build the blog library. If, for example, your company sells children's toys, you may find it appropriate to post every day, and your posts may range from 200 words to 1,000 words or more.

If you're selling financial-consulting services to a corporation, you may find that long-form blogs are most effective. These kinds of blogs take more time to research and write well, so unless you have a stable of writers working for you, it would be difficult to post new content every day.

If you're a team of one and just starting your blog, a good goal to shoot for is one blog a week. Any less and you'll probably not keep your readers' attention. There are too many other bloggers

8 John Rampton, "How Long Should My Blog Post Be?" *Forbes*, April 4, 2014.

out there competing for their time. When you are able to hit this goal consistently and get more comfortable at writing blogs, try to increase it to two posts a week.

I've found that blogging became easier for me as I completed more blogs. I became a more efficient writer. I also got in the habit of dedicating a little time each week to research new ideas and store them on my dashboard for future use. Somehow, knowing these potential post ideas were there made it easier for me to commit to writing more.

WHY INCREASE FREQUENCY?

Simple. Frequency is instrumental in helping your company build and maintain rapport with your constituents, while building your presence on the Web and in Google SEO so that you're always improving the odds of finding new constituents.

I've seen this practice help companies move from Page 10 in Google search results to Page 1 in a relatively short time. The caveat is that the content has to be good and your posts must be search engine optimized.

SHOULD BLOGS BE PROMOTIONAL?

Blatantly promotional, as in, a blog that spends 750 words telling readers why they should by your company's cleaning products over all others? No. That strategy will backfire, because your readers are probably in the learning stage of the engagement cycle when they're reading your blog, not the buying stage.

A good blog site is designed to persuade your constituents to trust you and eventually consider buying from you because your posts address their main questions, pain points and hopes. Readers don't come to blog sites to be sold.

I think writer and blogger Victor Ijidola said it well in a guest blog on problogger.net: "Millions of people visit various blogs every day to get tips that would help solve specific problems for them. If they begin to read your posts and notice that you're all about how to get their hard-earned cash, they mostly won't have a reason to give you their attention. And when they don't give you their attention, they're not in the right frame of mind to buy whatever you've got to sell. That's not to say you don't want to keep your readers aware of the products and services you sell."[9] Ijidola goes on in his post to suggest two ways to promote your services without blatantly selling.

You can also soft-sell by hyperlinking keywords in your blog to pages where your reader can learn more about your company's offering, and by adding your company's credentials and hyperlinks to key pages on your website at the end of every blog.

For example, I write a blog post for a software company whose readers are always interested in learning how they can reduce operational costs and the rates they are being charged

---

9   Victor Ijidola, "How to Advertise Your New Business In Blog Posts Without Looking Too Promotional," www.problogger.net/archives/2015/01/23/how-to-advertise-your-new-business-in-blog-posts-without-looking-too-promotional/, Jan. 23, 2015.

by carriers to deliver their packages. One post, "Five Keys to Reduce Dimensional Rating Costs," was written as a how-to checklist to help companies identify hidden operational issues that were resulting in unexpected shipping back charges from their carriers.

The post shared ideas to eliminate these operational problems and also suggested adding regional carriers as a way to reduce shipping costs. This post pulled six times above the normal click rate on the company's sponsored Linkedin page and outperformed all the blogs we had posted up to that point.

The company I was writing for is not a regional carrier; it provides the software on which all the carriers are loaded. This blog, about 1,000 words in length, did not promote the company's shipping software in the body of the post. It did, however, contain hyperlinks from key phrases that were part of the company's SEO strategy and its product offering. It also included a close that invited the reader to confer with the company:

"As a leading provider of carrier agnostic shipping solutions, ADSI's shipping software solution includes a large carrier library of national, regional, postal and international carriers. Please contact us today to explore how a carrier-agnostic shipping system can help you combat rising shipping charges."

To read the blog post and see how it was formatted, visit: www.smartshippingmadeeasy.com/five-tips-to-minimize-dimensional-rating-costs/

WHAT ABOUT SHARING OTHER PEOPLE'S POSTS?

This is another way to increase your own blog site's posting frequency, but keep the following in mind:

If you do choose to share another post, you still need to "keep the conversation going" with your reader. This can be done by writing an introductory paragraph about why you thought the post might be interesting to your readers. It's also good to engage your readers by asking them a question about the post you're sharing. This keeps the relationship with you as the top priority.

Be careful about the frequency with which you reshare posts. If you're sharing other's posts more than your own, you're running the risk of weakening your rapport with your constituents. If you're pressured for time and sharing posts as a means to keep new content on your blog, readers will sense this.

Another way to add longer posts is to interview guest experts. Sometimes the interview you conduct with an expert is good enough to stand as a post in itself.

TIPS FOR CREATING A FULL SCHEDULE OF BLOG POSTS

One way to build a schedule is to reserve a part of your attention to what's going on in your company and industry and keep a running list. For example:

- Set aside ten minutes a day to brainstorm blog topics.

- Bookmark articles or posts that you like for future reference.
- Ask your co-workers for blog ideas.
- Scan your competitor's blogs.
- Read trade journals and note interesting topics.
- Use case studies as a way to position a problem/solution.
- Invite others to write a post.
- Look for relevant industry surveys.
- Interview thought leaders whether they're in your company or work elsewhere.
- Reshare other interesting blogs.
- Take one of your white papers and break it down into a series of short blogs.
- Summarize new trends that you've seen at a recent industry event or trade show.
- Feature a Q&A session with customers, key employees, industry experts.
- Read LinkedIn, Twitter and other social media channels to reshare where it makes sense or get new ideas.

Idea generation is the beginning. Some of these examples will require more work, while others can be turned into a blog relatively easily. I build a blog calendar in which I mix the easy to-dos with the harder to-dos.

Five

How to Write Case Studies

"You can't sell anything if you can't tell anything."

— Beth Comstock

Case studies have been around for a long time, but the fact is they are still one of the most influential and versatile content marketing pieces you can invest in. People buy from people. They love stories about how someone they could identify with solved a problem or achieved success. No matter how great your sales literature is, your product videos are, or your product specs rank among your competitors, the fact remains – people buy from people. Case studies go a long way toward warming up a cold prospect into an engaged prospect and potential buyer. They build credibility.

However, case studies don't usually happen overnight and almost never do they fall into place according to your production plans, so it's good to have a few in the queue at a time. I am usually speaking with the sales team on an ongoing basis and keeping a pulse on at least six to ten companies that look like potential candidates.

GETTING STARTED

Following are some tips to kick off your own case study project list and keep it moving:

- **Work with senior management on the sales or service side to identify good customers.** This conversation can also include discussions with your salespeople, as they are often very aware of who will be willing to talk with you.

- **Ask for an introduction by the person who has the most influence with that particular case study.** This means asking the salesperson to ask the customer first – then let them know you're going to call them. In some cases, it may be the salesperson close to the account or the account manager. In some cases, it may be a project manager or senior management.

- **Introduce yourself via email and phone call.** Keep your original introducers in the loop; copy them on that initial introduction email so they know you've reached out. Keep them posted along with short updates of how the piece is coming along.

- **Ask for an interview.** And when they commit, send questions ahead of time so they can prepare. I use the following questions:

- Background of company/organization/person
- What was the business challenge they were trying to solve? What were some of the outcomes they were trying to eliminate?
- What options did they consider and why did they choose the choice?
- What was the process for implementation (if applicable) and were there any surprises?
- What benefits are they achieving with the new solution/service?

- **Once you complete the interview, create an outline or draft** of the case study based on the customer's comments and any additional material you'd like to include such as more detailed descriptions of the solution, your own company's role, quotes from your team, etc.
  - At this point, it's a good idea to show the draft to your internal team to verify what was said.
  - Share the first draft with your customer and encourage them to clarify any misconceptions or add other details they feel are important.
  - Once you incorporate everyone's changes, you're ready to go to final layout and publication.

- **Get final sign-off and thank your customer.** At this point, I send the final case study, with a permission form, to the customer. This gives them one more chance to make any last edits. I also make it a point to send them some sort of thank you, appropriate to their company policy, for their participation.

Written case studies take time but they're well worth it. As discussed earlier, they offer an excellent way to build credibility for your company and products, whether in a sales kit, on your website or as an article.

In many cases, the written case study can also serve as the basis for a video script. Of course you have to get the customer's buy-in, but they're often more willing to participate when they know the background research is already done. All that remains is shooting the footage and making sure they see it before it is finalized.

Six

How to Write a White Paper

"Don't write white papers stained with your sales pitch."

— ZACHARY JEANS

White papers are popular marketing tools, particularly for companies selling complex products or solutions. In my experience, they are one of the most effective content marketing tools a company can invest in.

WHAT EXACTLY IS A WHITE PAPER?

At this point, you might be saying, "Great, but what is a white paper?" Good question. Search the Internet for the origin or definition of a white paper and you'll find a range of answers. The truth is, there is no standard definition. It's a nebulous term whose meaning can be interpreted in many different ways.

Merriam Webster Dictionary says a white paper is "1) a government report on any subject; *especially*: a British publication that is usually less extensive than a blue book or 2) a detailed or authoritative report."

Investopedia defines a white paper as "an informational document issued by a company to promote or highlight the features of a solution, product or service."

Businessdictionary.com defines a white paper as "a marketing tool in the form of information on the technology underlying a complex product or system and on how it will benefit the customer."

The best definition I've found, based on the kinds of white papers I'm asked to write, is that of white paper expert Michael Stelzner: "A white paper is a persuasive essay that uses facts and logic to promote a certain product, service, or viewpoint. The content of a white paper provides useful information for business people seeking to understand an issue, solve a problem, or make a decision."[10]

Savvy companies have extended the scope of their white papers beyond focusing on informing and persuading their readers about a particular product or service. One client I work with, for example, has built up an extensive library of white papers by reporting on business trends for its customers. This client sells a financial technology platform and writes plenty of content about the value of the kind of technology it has pioneered.

---

10   Michael A. Stelzner, *Writing White Papers: How to Capture Readers and Keep Them Engaged,* WhitePaperSource Publishing, 2006.

But beyond that, the company also wanted to become a "go to" source for its customers to catch up on trends in the financial industry to watch, so it now publishes a series of educational white papers that summarize trends, provide survey results and focus on topics beyond the technology platform it provides.

This has proven to be extremely effective in convincing prospective customers that the company is an expert in the financial industry so they can trust its technology platform. This has also worked well to build an ongoing relationship with its existing clients and keep the brand in front of them for future purchases.

PROMOTIONAL OR EDUCATIONAL?

Some companies write promotional content and call it a white paper. Others provide informative or educational content that is completely unbiased toward any company or solution.

For purposes of this book on generating marketing content, a white paper is an informative document that provides the reader with knowledge on a specific topic, presented by your company as a thought leader. In this way it is biased in that it presents your company's point of view regarding best practices, best solutions, etc. But it doesn't go as far as focusing solely on, or blatantly promoting, your company or brand as the solution to choose.

Paula Heikell

WHAT WHITE PAPERS ARE NOT

Although it's true that there is no standard definition of what a white paper is or how it should be constructed, there are some characteristics of what it should not be if your goal is to establish trust with your reader. Following are some guidelines to keep in mind:

- **Don't be overly promotional.** The best white papers inform and persuade an audience by presenting a solid business case based on facts. After presenting the problem and solution, they then offer the reader a chance to learn more about their company, product or service in an unobtrusive manner.

- **Don't try to use a white paper for a sales brochure or vice versa.** You need both, but they play different roles in the buyer's educational journey. If you attract a reader's attention by marketing a white paper and the reader learns it is really just a sales brochure touting why your product is best and why they should buy it, you'll actually run the risk of offending and losing that prospect.

- **Choose the right voice.** White papers are often read by executives or senior management members who are tasked with making a business decision. They rely on white papers as a quick study to find what they need to know to make a well-balanced choice. The right voice here is not too familiar, nor should it be too academic. Write in a direct, concise style that conveys the issues and facts in a straightforward manner.

ELEMENTS OF A WHITE PAPER

Most white papers are structured around a problem/solution formula. Good white papers are laid out in a logical sequence.

INTRODUCTION

This is the place where you set the stage for the entire paper. First you provide readers with a quick summary of what to expect and help them decide if they are members of the intended audience. The introduction should include a succinct summary of the challenge, the solution and how the reader will benefit. Stelzner defines this section as the first page formula with four elements:

- Identify the reader.
- Summarize the challenge.
- Summarize the solution.
- State the goal.

He also offers a great explanation about what these elements should do:

"The four steps of the first page formula are very important and serve distinct purposes. Revealing the ideal reader quickly filters the audience by describing who will benefit from the white paper. Explaining key challenges builds affinity with readers by highlighting issues they care about and also further filters out those readers who are not facing similar challenges. Providing a brief introduction to the solution helps readers know what to look forward to in the white paper. Clearly stating the goal helps readers understand what they will learn by reading the white paper."[11]

Here's an example:

I was asked to write a white paper designed to inform private equity firms about how they could improve their fundraising activities. The goal, of course, was to educate the audience on the opportunity they had; the challenges in taking advantage of it; and how the right technology could resolve the challenge.

The paper was aimed at private equity firms that were still relying on traditional paper documents and postal mail methods to communicate with potential investors.

To set the stage, I focused on the turmoil in the financial markets and how it was causing investors to look to specialist private equity firms for better returns. The paper went on to discuss how this shift could be a boon to specialist firms – provided they could move quickly to reach these clients while the window of opportunity was open. It also described how firms using paper and postal mail processes may not be in a position to act quickly enough.

---

11 Michael A. Stelzner, *Writing White Papers: How to Capture Readers and Keep Them Engaged*, WhitePaperSource Publishing, 2006 p. 62.

In this case, I wrote the introduction in the following way:

- Cited industry trends that I had found by researching multiple news sources.
- Quoted an expert to reinforce these trends.
- Created the hook: opportunity for certain firms to win new clients because of the market turmoil.
- Cited the urgency in reaching and communicating with new clients.

I provided a hint of a solution by telling the audience that new technology was available to help them quickly reach these investors.

NEXT SECTION: BUILD THE BUSINESS CASE

This section should go into greater detail about the key elements of the issue and inform the reader about ways to resolve these issues.

In the case of the fundraising white paper, this meant creating a checklist of six challenges smaller firms faced in responding quickly to interested investors.

For example:

- It took time for staff to print the large "pitch books" and mail them to investors.
- There was little means to track the books and determine if they were received, opened or read.

- Using email to send pitch books was cumbersome and difficult to track.
- Traditional mail and email lacked security.
- Communicating with investors and responding quickly was not always guaranteed.

I created bullet points of each of these challenges and used them to explain how the right kind of technology could be used to eliminate them. At this point, the benefits of this technology were presented as basic features or components of an ideal solution. Each bullet also explained the business benefit of these features in terms of how the readers' operations would improve if they had access to them.

Although the features and benefits are presented in a neutral tone, they are, in fact, all to be found in the company's technology platform. This approach worked, because the company was in fact an early pioneer of the technology and had set the stage for how it took shape, even as other solutions became available.

BENEFITS BEYOND THE INITIAL ISSUE

Another tactic that we chose to include in the white paper was to add examples of how this new technology could be deployed to improve other aspects of the private equity firm's operations beyond fundraising. This included specific example benefits it delivered in other areas of operations, including acquisitions, portfolio management and managing the sales of assets.

In this way, the paper provided a good overview of basic requirements to be considered for this technology.

BRANDING YOUR WHITE PAPER

In the above example, the company's product and brand did not appear until the back cover of the paper. It was written in such a way that the company could present its thought leadership in a neutral yet persuasive manner that allowed the reader to formulate his or her own opinions. But it also included the company's credentials and contact information when the reader was ready to talk.

OTHER KINDS OF WHITE PAPERS

The example I cited above was focused on a product and it worked very well for the company's marketing goal – to generate leads from the fundraising decision makers of a private equity firm. It was structured around a straightforward problem/solution format. You can also add many other elements to the paper to make it more engaging for the reader, such as:

- Checklists of key elements to look for in the white paper (solutions to problems)
- Examples/case studies of successes or failures
- History or background that has led to the current situation you're solving
- Market trends and expert predictions
- Statistics, charts to build your case

The best white papers, in my opinion, also provide other non-promotional information that helps give the reader a perspective of the issue it is trying to solve. For example,

- A white paper featuring "X Best Practices to Develop an Effective Multilingual Online Retail Website" may include background information about the size and growth of the international e-commerce world. It may also cite some examples of failures by companies that failed because they did not follow these practices.

- Another kind of paper featuring practical advice on how to choose the right accounting software system may include basic tips, common assumptions and gaps in the process that result in a less-than-ideal decision. Again, this isn't promotional content, but the "war stories" of actual buyers. Some of this material can come from other articles (properly referenced). If you're the software company writing it, some of it can come from learned experiences from your customers.

- White papers discussing emerging trends and how readers can position their businesses to be prepared for them are also popular. For example, many companies are grappling with the "Bring Your Own Device" world and how to address it in their own workplace. You can research this topic by industry, by statistics and by technology recommendations on the Internet and provide your readers with invaluable background information that will build your company's credibility.

FINDING BACKGROUND MATERIAL

Some companies have deep resources on which to build white papers, but many do not have the staff, time or resources. Also, projects like white papers tend to start with just an idea in a conversation, with very little background to help you get started.

If you find yourself in this position, don't despair. There is much more support material out there than you'd initially think. Sources can include:

- Company-generated information such as the website, presentations, product requirements documents, brochures, company profiles, etc.
- Business articles, analyst reports, statistics
- Interviews with company thought leaders
- Interviews with industry peers
- Competitor information
- Industry associations

The first place I start, if possible, is in interviewing key stakeholders in the company as well as outside expert sources. If you don't have access to outside experts, consider contacting the director of your company's industry associations. He or she can often help by suggesting topics and also making introductions.

Talking first to internal or external experts is the most efficient way to find out what the most important topics are and prevent yourself from spending hours of research in areas or on topics that will not apply.

For example, one white paper project I was working on focused on a new design for crutches. The client provided me with plenty of background information on traditional crutches as well as a list of medical specialists and patients who were willing to be interviewed.

My first call was to the orthopedic specialist who had made the decision to provide patients with the new crutches. In the space of an hour, he was able to quickly point out the most important aspects of why he chose to adopt the crutches and the benefits they were benchmarking with patients. My next call was to a physical therapist.

The point is, after reading through the background materials, without talking with these medical professionals, it would have been easy to focus on the wrong aspects of the product and the audience (orthopedic specialists and medical clinic managers) in building the case for the crutches.

The interviews saved me from doing further research on the less important aspects of the problem/solution and helped me focus in on the key aspects to cover to craft a compelling white paper much more quickly.

TITLES AND SUBTITLES

I usually begin with a working title and don't worry too much about it until I'm reaching the final stages of the white paper. I also try to come up with a few titles and test them with the product managers or stakeholders to make sure they are compelling and resonate with the readers.

I don't put it off because the title isn't important – rather, it's because it is so important. As Robert W. Bly, author of *The White Paper Marketing Handbook* notes, "Whether prospects eagerly send for your white paper or pass it by is determined largely by the title."[12]

For me, the best titles come to mind once I am nearly finished with the written piece.

Following are some other recommendations to keep in mind:

- **Use Google to get ideas**. When you put in the keywords you used to search for source articles, what titles came up? Which were most interesting?

- **Use keywords**. Ask your marketing team what they are and use them in your title and subtitle to ensure that they will come up in searches once the white paper is published. For more explanation, refer to Chapter 11.

- **Titles with numbers work very well**. "Six Tips to …" or "Four Reasons You Need …" always seem to perform well in email campaigns.

---

12   Robert Bly, *The White Paper Marketing Handbook*, Mason, Ohio: Thomson Higher Education, 2006.

- **Short titles also work well**. They have higher search results when the keywords are embedded in them. They're harder to write, but pay off in the response rate.

- **A series can be effective**. For example, one project I worked on was a four-part series. If the topic had been contained in one white paper, it would have been 25 pages, much longer than today's readers are inclined to read. Creating a series of four shorter papers enabled the reader to digest the content in shorter form and look for more to come. It also multiplied the company's opportunity to attract prospective clients by a factor of four, and readers contacted the company to receive copies of the other white papers in the series.

REFERENCES

Cite your references. Be accurate. If you're not certain how to cite references properly, seek guidance from reference sources such as *The Associated Press Stylebook* or *The Chicago Manual of Style*. Style standards can be confusing and can also change, so I often seek the advice of an experienced copy editor.

SUMMARY

I love white papers almost as much as I love newsletters and case studies. They have a long shelf life and the content within them can be used as teasers in multiple e-campaigns to capture readers' attention and their email addresses.

To be really effective, however, keep a few things in mind:

- **Provide useful information**. If you use the "bait and switch" tactic by attracting prospects with the promise that they're going to learn something and then present them with a sales pitch, you'll lose them.

- **Shorter papers seem to appeal to business readers**. I've found that four to six pages is a good length, but again, there is no definitive answer. It's best to test the market.

- **Keep your topic on task**. Check yourself along the way. Did you deliver the content that you promised or diverge from the topic? Is it too wordy and does it lose the readers' attention? Is it written at the right level for the audience you're seeking?

- **If your topic is not getting clicks, test a new title**. I often survey the Internet to see how a particular topic is being written about by others. By searching the key words or phrases for your topic, you can find other examples of titles that may generate ideas to improve yours.

The good news is, if you've never written a white paper before, you get to be more efficient with every one you write. I'd recommend Michael Stelzner's book, *Writing White Papers*, for a deeper dive into this important piece of marketing content.

Seven

How to Write a Press Release

"The law of publicity – the birth of a brand is achieved with publicity, not advertising."

— Al Ries & Laura Ries

Press releases represent another useful content marketing tool, as long as they are written in a way that the desired audience wants to read them. Press releases can cover a variety of topics to generate publicity for your company/brand and build awareness with known and yet-to-be discovered followers. You can write about:

- **General company news**. For example, if your company wins a business award, opens a new facility, supports a charity or cause, all of these topics can be used to build exposure for the company.

- **Product news**. Announce new products, product rebates, recalls, upgrades, etc. It's always good to provide photos with product releases to increase the likelihood of getting placement.

- **Employee news**. New key employees or changes in executive management are good topics. Again, it's good to include a photo and bio.

- **Event-related news**. If your company is exhibiting its latest products or speaking at an industry event, write about it. This lets the editors who are attending know you'll be there and sets the stage for a potential interview.

- **Launches**. If you're launching a new website, a new campaign or other initiative such as supporting Earth Day in a certain way, write about it.

Where does the source material for the release come from? It depends on the size of the organization, but as a general rule of thumb, there is usually a lead person who you can interview to get started.

For example, the CEO and/or senior manager of operations may be the source to tell you the important points about a new facility opening, its impact on the business, etc. You may need to talk to the product and sales group leaders to get the most important facts on an upcoming product release. The marketing department will provide you with background information for marketing events or launches.

STRUCTURE OF A PRESS RELEASE

You will find a variety of press release formats when you search the Internet. Following are some basic guidelines.

WHAT TO INCLUDE IN A PRESS RELEASE

Headline. This is the title of your release. It needs to be written in a compelling way that gives readers a sense of what the release is about and pique their interest. Note, good headlines can be tricky to write. I usually start with a working title and finalize it after the release is finalized.

Lead paragraph. This is the place you'll summarize your story. I think of this paragraph as the what, when, where, why section. You're writing this to show reporters, editors and others why they should keep reading.

Nut paragraph. Think of this paragraph as the place to share a fuller explanation of the story you've created in the first paragraph. Content in this paragraph or paragraphs should be useful information that rounds out the story. If you're announcing a new product that reduces costs or saves time, this could be the place for a more detailed explanation of how the product does this.

Quote(s). It's good to include quotes in the story, especially if they're written in a personable style that actually sounds the way people speak. You can use a company spokesperson, a customer or other appropriate person to comment. Make sure it sounds real and it truly adds to the story. Quotes can also be very powerful in speaking to the strengths of your product or service, without having to sound like you're selling. A well-done quote gets the point across much more effectively.

Background information. You can add background information in subsequent paragraphs, but view it as nice to have and not necessary to the release.

"About" Boilerplate. Include a short paragraph about your organization or company, including contact information, key words and links to your website. This should summarize who you are and your organization's mission or focus.

There is, of course, no singular way to think about press release structure, so it's a good idea to search the Internet on the topic of press release format. You'll find a wide range of guidelines that may be helpful to you.

CREATING THE MOST EFFECTIVE NEWS RELEASE

Following are some recommendations to create good releases:

- **Follow the news lead formula – who, what, when, where and why**. This formula has been the standard for years, and despite the evolution from print to online media, editors and media experts recommend that companies follow this structure.

- **Write in third person.**

- **Keep your primary message clear.** What is the main thought you want reporters and your audience to take away with them? Get to it fast, and state it succinctly to keep the reader's attention. Too many messages water down your release and also potentially confuse the reader as to what is most important.

- **The press release should be written in the order of most important information followed by less important information.** This is useful for getting key content across quickly before the reader starts skimming. It also means that if a publication uses a shorter version of your release, the most salient information will likely make the cut.

- **Keep it short.** Longer releases of multiple pages are not necessarily viewed favorably. The PR Newswire recommends a length of 400 to 500 words for greatest effect.

- **Be careful of jargon.** It's very easy to slip into technical jargon that is commonly understood within the company but not usually clear to the broader audience of journalists and editors. They are not experts like you. Take the time to replace jargon with clearly understood terminology.

- **Write with keywords.** Make sure you've identified one or two keywords or phrases that readers are likely to search for and embed them in the title, the subtitle, in a couple of places in the body copy without being overly redundant, and in the actual URL when you post it to your website.

- **Add photos, videos or multimedia** to create greater interest.

THE INTEREST FACTOR

As you're creating the press release, it's critical to put yourself in the position of the reader. Pretend you know nothing about your company and ask yourself, "If I were the reader, why should I care?" That's one litmus test of determining whether your press release is newsworthy.

Another test is to take your release through the following questions provided by the PR Newswire:

- Is your angle different from other similar stories and/or does it offer a unique perspective?
- Does your message contain new information, even if it's about an older subject?
- Can your message bring light to a problem or issue, or, conversely, provide a resolution to a problem or issue?
- Does your message carry emotional weight with bloggers and other readers?
- Does your message involve or quote a famous or high-powered person?
- Does your message impact the geographical location or environment of the reader base?

If you can affirm your story with one or some of the above, you've likely got a newsworthy topic in hand.[13]

DISTRIBUTION OPTIONS

The best way to maximize exposure of your content is through multiple distribution channels. A combination may include:

- Your company's own editorial and marketing database
- Your website
- Your company newsletter
- Online service such as the PR Newswire or PRWeb
- Your social media accounts

It's important to note that while the first three channels will help you reach your constituents, it's a good idea to use an online service as well. This gets your content released to thousands of sites and also ensures that it is indexed by Google and will contribute to your page ranking in Google searches.

CREATE A PRESS KIT PAGE

It's also a good idea to create a press kit page designed to make it easier for editors or publications to get access to any information they need. Your press kit page should include:

---

13   "Writing and Formatting Tips for News Releases," PR Newswire Association, ireach.prnewswire.com/tips.aspx, 2014.

- **Company Story**. How did your business or organization get started? What is its focus?

- **Company Facts.** When did the company begin doing business and where is it located? Do you have multiple offices? What products do you make and sell? How many customers do you have and where are they located? These are a few examples, but you can also add other facts such as revenue, etc.

- **Logos and graphics in a variety of formats.** This will make it easier for publishers to work with your content. Options include high-quality, high-resolution graphics for online or print publications.

- **Bios.** Provide background on the key stakeholders in the company. This may include management as well as industry experts whose presence adds distinction to your company and brand.

- **Other press releases and articles.** Include articles, interviews, blog posts, inclusions of your company on other websites, etc., as a way to show people that your company is newsworthy and worth working with.

- **Additional content such as videos, awards, etc.** These are optional but if you have them, make sure to add them to the page.

Eight

How to Create a Newsletter

*"If we only talk about ourselves,
we'll never reach customers."*

—JOE PULIZZI

I have to confess that I absolutely love company newsletters. They are one of the most effective forms of marketing content a company or organization can produce, and they can go a long way in building brand awareness and customer loyalty for a relatively low cost.

Following are some recommendations to get you started.

STEP 1: ESTABLISH YOUR GOALS

The first step is to define the audience for your newsletter. If your company sells a product or service, it's most likely that your primary audience will include customers and prospects, but it may also include your partners, editorial press and professional groups. With this in mind, what is the goal behind the newsletter? You may have one or more goals such as to:

- Put a "face" on your company.
- Keep your customers informed.
- Build your brand.
- Announce new products or services.
- Upsell or cross-sell products to customers.
- Position your organization as a thought leader.
- Provide industry news.
- Generate leads and drive sales.
- Increase traffic to your website.

These are just a few examples of objectives; you may have others. You may even choose to use your newsletter to serve multiple objectives. That's fine, but just don't make the mistake of choosing too many. Your newsletter will become cluttered and your objective diluted. The most effective newsletters have a clearly defined mission and message, and clear expectations about what the newsletter should do.

That's why it's so important to take the time to define your goals. Once you do this, it's much easier to determine what kind of source material you need, who may be able to contribute, how the newsletter should be formatted and what metrics you'll use to track its effectiveness.

Promotional or Informational?

Again, this is going to vary based on your specific organization, market and mission. Experts such as Hubspot.com recommend maintaining a ratio of 10% promotional and 90% informational, although I think that can be adjusted, provided it does become largely promotional.

STEP 2: DETERMINE FREQUENCY

Should you send your newsletter quarterly, monthly, weekly or daily? Depends on your business and your market. For the B-to-B space I've worked in, I like the frequency of monthly newsletters, but only if I can be sure that we'll be able to keep up with the schedule.

Good newsletters are almost like a "comfort" read for loyal subscribers. They get accustomed to receiving it and notice when an issue is skipped, so once you set an expectation for its circulation, don't mess with it without informing your audience. Don't skip an issue, even if you're pressed for time.

STEP 3: DELIVER THE CONTENT

Print or electronic? Or both? Electronic versions of newsletters have become mainstream these days, although I still receive printed newsletters from some companies. It's a question worth discussing, particularly if a large portion of your audience is not found on the Internet.

Companies that sell healthcare products to the aging population, for example, may find that a portion of their buyers may prefer printed newsletters, while the other portion will read them online. In these cases, both formats may be the best solution.

Nonetheless, most companies have migrated to electronic newsletters. Within that realm, you can structure the newsletter in several ways:

- As a traditional newsletter containing complete stories
- As a collection of short introductions with hyperlinks to the story, video, etc., on your website
- As a series of short introductory lead-ins that invite the reader to provide his or her email and download the full story

I've experimented with all of these formats to test which drives the greatest open-and-click rate. In the past, full stories with hyperlinks worked well, but the rapid adoption of mobile devices has changed that.

Much has been written about how extensively consumers shop, surf and generally read and do more than ever on their smartphones. It's also true in the B-to-B world, where it's easy to assume that buyers still sit in an office and use a desktop computer to do their jobs.

This is simply not true anymore. One company I work with has been tracking the steady migration of its readership from traditional desktop browsers to smartphone browsers. In five years, the portion of its subscribers who read the newsletter on a smartphone has increased from 10% to 65%.

It's important to keep this in mind as you shape your audience profile. True, you can choose mobile-enabled templates that resize the newsletter for whichever device the reader is using, but you still may need to tweak your headlines and the length of your content. Take a look at how your newsletters come across on desktops, tablets and smart devices before you hit the publish button.

HOW LONG SHOULD YOUR NEWSLETTER BE?

Some experts will say it depends on the frequency. Daily newsletters should be shorter than weeklies, which should be shorter than monthly newsletters. Other experts say it should be as long as it needs to be to provide value. I agree with both of these points, but there is a third element to consider – the shrinking attention spans of today's readers.

I like this advice by marketer Mad Mimi. It fits with what I see these days:

"I'd say your newsletter can be as long as you'd like but make sure your most important info goes up top. If your newsletter needs five minutes of uninterrupted attention by your readers, then you need to be comfortable knowing that most readers won't make it to the bottom. Also, if your newsletter is taking you hours to compose, it's probably too long."[14]

One of my colleagues calls the way that we read on our phones "snacking on data" and I'd have to agree with him. For this reason, I'd lead toward creating a newsletter with a clean, simple design that offers short articles with hyperlinks to more detailed content. The key is to write eye-catching headlines and intro paragraphs that make readers want to keep reading and let your newsletter design give them the choice of how they want to read.

NEWSLETTER SOURCES

You can put a newsletter together pretty quickly if you're working on content in parallel tracks as suggested in Chapter 2. If this is the case, you should have a collection of the latest blog posts, case studies and press releases that can serve as the basis for articles. You can also make it easier by occasionally featuring a guest post or article.

I'd also recommend creating some standard categories in which you can draw on others to help you generate content. Here are some, for example, that are easy to write, short in length and can be gathered in advance for several upcoming issues:

---

14   "Answers to Top Ten Email Marketing Questions," www.madmimi. com, Sept. 3, 2013.

- **A product FAQ section**. Your product or customer support team can probably give you a list of topics/features, complete with copy that they've already created.

- **Customer service section**. There are likely a series of common questions that the service team routinely encounters. This is a good place to share the answers.

- **Events section**. This can be a short article on upcoming trade shows and what the company will be exhibiting or speaking about.

- **Partner news**. If your company works with multiple partners, you can rotate short promotions or product updates, written by the partner.

- **Meet our employees**. This is an excellent way to add a human element to your brand.

- **Welcome to new customers**. Some of my clients love this idea, while others don't necessarily want to let any competitors who are reading the newsletter know who their customers are.

- **Tip or idea of the month**. Customers always tell me that they like to hear what their peers are doing and learn from them.

TRACK YOUR ACTIVITY

Depending on the size of your company, you may already have an email platform in place to send out the e-newsletter and track readers' actions. If so, that's great. Your marketing team should be able to give you some metrics about readership, click activity, downloads, etc.

If you don't, it is worth talking to an e-marketing agency or specialist before you begin. There is a broad range of tools available to conduct your own program, or you may opt to outsource it.

Either way, monitor your results and don't be afraid to experiment with your newsletter's format to see if it improves your results.

Above all, have fun. Newsletters are usually not expected to be as formal in tone and style as other business communications. They give us some room to show the human side of the company. Sometimes, that's the element that drives up readership numbers.

Nine

Interviewing Tips

*"Everything in writing begins with language. Language
begins with listening."*

—JEANETTE WINTERSON

I love interviewing people. It infuses raw energy into every project and gives it life. But many times, I work with entrepreneurs, executives and industry experts whose time is extremely limited. These people want to share their passion and ideas with their constituents, but they're constantly juggling a jam-packed schedule. However, I've found that they'll make time for you if you can prove to them you'll use it well.

It used to be that interviewing was a skill most often associated with researchers, writers or media hosts, but with the rise of the Internet and the constant quest for new content, we're all becoming interviewers now. I was fortunate; I studied and practiced interviewing, on and off camera, as part of my college coursework.

If you have time to take an interviewing class or workshop, I'd highly recommend it. Not only did these classes give me a good foundation of the principles, but they also helped me overcome the sheer DREAD I had of seeing or hearing my recorded self. Going through that exercise – in a class where the stakes are not high – also had the effect of instantly correcting the ums, ahs and other quirks that you may not even be aware you have.

If you don't have time to take a class, you might be learning to interview "on the job." Don't worry; you'll be on your way to being an interview expert by adhering to some very basic guidelines. After conducting hundreds of interviews – and watching others at work – I think almost anyone can become a good interviewer by following a few best practices.

Over time, I've learned that short, 20- to 30-minute interviews, scheduled in advance, will usually yield enough content for several different marketing pieces. Also during the interview, my sources will share great ideas beyond the scope of the initial topic that are perfect for thought leadership articles, a series of blog posts, etc.

This is where recording comes in. Interview transcripts are, in my opinion, the key to building a rich content library. They're idea builders. Many times, by reviewing the transcripts, I discover great "nuggets" that were mentioned in passing during the interview but turn out to be the tip of the iceberg for another full-fledged, highly interesting content campaign.

Ensuring that you've captured all of the potential ideas generated in an interview is very simple to do, especially with today's conference call recording capabilities. Of course, it is vital to let your sources know up front that you're recording the interview. I assure them that I don't share the recordings with anyone. I use them solely for fact checking and to make sure I haven't missed any critical aspect of our conversation.

This approach is well accepted. Many times, my sources appreciate the efficient use of their time and, once they see how the work turns out, look forward to the interviews to share ideas they know are important, but never seem to have the time to write down themselves.

SEVEN INTERVIEWING TIPS TO DRIVE GOOD CONTENT GENERATION

Plan ahead. Quite often I interview industry professionals who are at the top of their game, in an industry that is new to me. Without fail, these are highly engaged individuals with full calendars, so I don't expect them to be available "same day."

I've found I get the best results by preparing a short email to introduce myself and a brief synopsis of the project. I also tell them how much I value their participation, and inquire if they're available for a short interview. I often include a few samples of my other work to give them an idea of what they can expect. Most often, they'll respond with a clear yes or no, and indicate the best way to proceed.

Tell your interviewee what is going to happen, when, and make sure you follow through. Once I get a "yes," I respond with a huge thank you and a plan to send a short summary of questions in advance of the scheduled interview. This can be done a week or a few days in advance, but it's important to get the questions to interviewees when you promise so they have time to formulate their thoughts. It sets a precedent of professionalism and shows the participant you respect his or her time.

Create a handful of open-ended questions. Do your research. You don't have to become an expert, but dig deep enough so that you're able to pose relevant questions. Don't use yes/no questions. Instead, create open-ended questions that invite the interviewee to share his or her opinions, observations and predictions.

For example, rather than asking, "Do you think cloud-based technology is going to change your business?" ask, "How do you think cloud-based technology is going to change your business?"

Avoid being vague. Sometimes people respond better when you ask, "Can you tell me the three main factors that were key to your company's success?" rather than, "What has made your company so successful?" You'll have to play with this. Some people are more comfortable and accustomed to being interviewed than others.

Do your homework. The Internet makes it easier than ever to gather background facts on just about anyone. Nonetheless, I've listened to interviews in which the questioner has not taken the time to read up on his or her guest in advance. That's the kiss of death. If your guest says, "You could have found this on our website, but…" you know he or she knows you're not as prepared as you should be.

Start by providing a quick summary of the project, and then ask the interviewee to share his or her own background before diving into the more focused questions. This shows your interest and it's a great way to warm up the process.

For example, I was preparing to interview the founder of a company who was very well known in his industry and in Manhattan social circles – someone with decades of publicity behind him. I was a bit nervous.

Doing my homework helped. I noted in his online bio that we both attended the same university. I mentioned this at the outset of our call, and it opened the door to a lively conversation. The key here is that your background research is important, but equally important, your interest must be genuine.

Listen more, talk less. You know those media interviews in which the host asks a long-winded question and follows it with a series of his own insights before allowing his guest to talk? That may be fine for TV talk shows in which the host is trying to build a persona for himself. It is definitely not the tactic to take when you're trying to learn something from your guest.

In fact, I view my job not as a chance to show what I know, but to get my guest to share what he or she knows, in his or her own words. I view it as the 85-15 rule. If I'm doing my job well, my guest is talking 85% of the time and I'm talking 15% of the time.

Remember, no one is expecting you to be the expert. You do, however, need to be a credible interviewer. Your goal, in preparation, is to do enough background research to be able to formulate relevant questions that will yield meaningful answers.

That's the beauty of preparing and sending your questions in advance. I always ask my interviewees if my questions are a good starting point or if they have suggestions. They'll usually tell you if you're on the mark, and also if their expertise doesn't apply to certain questions.

Be respectful. Respect your interviewees' time and willingness to share their knowledge with you. Ask them if it is okay to check back in the future. Depending on the project, I also offer to let them preview their quotes before I finalize the document.

You'd be surprised how many times contributors will realize what they said in the interview came across differently than they intended, even when I've captured their exact words. Their edits usually have to do with the style in which they spoke or validating facts. The overall result is an improved document. It's the right thing to do in this case. This is business writing, not journalism or muckraking.

Follow up. Send a thank you note after the interview. Let your guest know what will happen next and when. When your writing project is complete and published or posted, be sure to send him or her a copy.

Following these steps has yielded, for me, many productive conversations that were enjoyable and informative for both parties. It also has helped me build a network of enthusiastic experts who are willing to participate in future projects. Have fun!

Ten

Plan Ongoing Content Generation

"Stop selling. Start helping."

— Zig Ziglar

I've found content generation to be a common challenge for virtually all the companies I work with, large and small. But truthfully, it's easy to talk yourself into thinking it's harder than it really is.

Many marketers overwhelm themselves by downloading multitudes of surveys, blog posts and white papers from the Internet. They think their writing has to be perfect and give up before they even get started. Another diversion is to fixate on finding just the right technology platform to launch their campaigns. The fact remains, once the platform is up and running, many of us still have a hard time generating enough content to build a schedule of campaigns.

It doesn't have to be that difficult. Following are some simple, practical tips that can work very well if you're struggling to get started.

MAKE CONTENT GENERATION A TOP PRIORITY

Content generation is still relatively new for many companies and is often assigned to an employee who already has a full-time job with other responsibilities. Not only are they being asked to take on additional work, but it's work that involves writing – a professional skill, and one that many people absolutely dread. Consequently, content generation tasks fall to the bottom of their to-do list.

A better approach is to hire a writer, either as staff or as an outsourced professional, whose primary focus is to create content ideas, gather background materials, and maintain a calendar for you. If they're a professionally trained business writer, they'll have the background/training/skill set to do all of this very efficiently. In the end, this is the best and most cost-effective way to ensure that you'll consistently have fresh, high-quality content to build a long-term marketing content calendar.

MAINTAIN A REGULAR BUT SIMPLE SCHEDULE FOR CONTENT GATHERING

If you're the designated content generator, take a few minutes at least once a week to look ahead and do some quick, simple research to identify potential topics. Ask your colleagues for their ideas. Jot down ideas on a white board. Bookmark useful website pages. Print articles and store them in a "research" file.

Also, try to set aside one hour, two times a week for research and line up one or two interviews (recorded) per week with product managers or other company experts. If you can achieve this, you'll have plenty of background material that can be stored and retrieved to create new campaigns.

Like I said, these are basic steps, but they're very effective in building a successful content generation program. Get these few components of your program nailed down, and you'll be surprised at how rapidly your content library will grow.

SCHEDULE SHORT CHECK-INS WITH YOUR CONTRIBUTORS

The trick here is to keep your contributors informed of what you're doing with the information they've given you. I always make sure to send them the final versions of the written piece, thank them for their time, and encourage them to publicize the piece for their own use.

I also try to reciprocate by sharing something of interest to them. This can be a short, "thought you might be interested" email from time to time. I also, where it makes sense, send them a note when I have something coming up that they may be interested in contributing to – because the publicity is just as good for them as it is for my client.

For tips on getting your content gathering idea machine rolling, see Chapter 2.

Eleven

How to Write Web Pages

"The Internet is becoming the town square for the global village of tomorrow."

— Bill Gates

Whatever you write, it will likely find its way to the Internet, often in the form of a Web page. Whether the readers you're targeting find your Web pages depends on how well they are set up to be found. For best results, follow basic steps to formatting your Web page writing for Internet search engines. But first, let's go over the actual definition of SEO and the meaning of keywords.

SEO

Webopedia offers a good definition:

"SEO is short for search *engine* optimization or *search engine* optimizer. Search engine optimization is a methodology of strategies, techniques and tactics used to increase the amount of visitors to a <u>website</u> by obtaining a high-ranking placement in the search results page of a <u>search engine</u> (<u>SERP</u>) – including Google, Bing, Yahoo and other search engines."

In common-speak, it's a way to format your content so that it appears on "Page 1" in page rankings in reader searches.

KEYWORDS

Keywords sum up the content on your Web page or blog post and act as a shortcut that allows a search engine such as Google to match your page to a reader's search query.

Many large companies have likely already established an SEO strategy and can provide you with the list of keywords that they've targeted, so it's a good idea to ask your marketing team if this is already in place.

However, for every company that has already established an SEO strategy, there are just as many who haven't. If it's your job to also come up with the keywords, it may take some time. Again, a good place to start is to interview your company's product knowledge and industry experts, which may include the founder, product manager, sales staff and customer service staff.

Most companies begin by identifying keywords and optimizing their content for Google since it is the leading search engine in the U.S. If this is the case, it's a good idea to become familiar with

Google Analytics tools. I don't pretend to be an SEO expert, but I find it very helpful to use Google's tools to research keywords before we actually begin using them.

For example, let's say you come up with a list of keywords that are commonly used to describe the product you sell. You can enter these keywords in a Google form and see how frequently they show up in user searches or, in some cases, whether they show up much at all. You can use this information to decide if they are the right words to use or if what you've chosen is too obscure and try other combinations until you round out your list.

It's important to note that if you're writing content that will be localized for other languages and countries, Google is not the best tool to use. The search engines and the phrases will be different and the keywords that consumers use in other languages are probably not literal translations.

As one blog post on this topic pointed out, "Mitsubishi discovered that one of its more popular sports utility vehicles, the Pajero, failed in the Spanish-speaking market because its name literally means 'a crazy man who pleasures himself repeatedly into unconsciousness.' Purdue Chicken made a subtler error when it translated its famous slogan, 'It takes a tough man to make a tender chicken.' In Spanish, the slogan read, 'It takes a hard man to make a chicken affectionate.'"[15]

---

15 "Does Your Brand Work in the Spanish Language Market?" Merrill Corporation blog.

As you can see, if you're optimizing your pages with keywords for international markets, it's best to work with a language translation company to make sure this is done right. Otherwise, you run the very real risk of not identifying the right keywords or phrases and not showing up in the search engines.

KEYWORD PLACEMENT IN WEB CONTENT

When you're writing content, the keywords or phrases should be embedded at multiple points in your page, post, description:

- In the URL of the post or Web page
- In the H1 and H2 tags
- A few times in the content – in the first paragraph, in the middle and then in the end

Your keywords should also be included in the meta description for each page or post. This is the content that comes up when your page shows up in a search. If you don't do it, Google fills in the details for you.

It can be easy to lose sight of the keyword process. I'd recommend keeping a spreadsheet or list of keywords and supporting information.

INCLUDING KEYWORDS IN CONTENT

This is a challenging topic because it requires you to think like your audience(s) and Internet search engines, and be careful to zoom in on those terms that truly attract the right people. If you don't take the time to learn how keywords work, you can waste inordinate amounts of time and money attracting the wrong people to your page or posts.

The truth is, the first few times I worked at this, I was overwhelmed by how much has to be taken into consideration. It requires a bit of a brain shift. My mind was not accustomed to writing in this formulaic manner, but it quickly adapted. Besides that, once I could compare the Web traffic results from pages that were not search engine optimized to those that were, I was convinced.

IF YOU DO NOT HAVE KEYWORDS TO START

For many small companies, the marketing department, whether it is one person or a small team, is the source for keyword research and, quite frequently, this step of identifying keywords is overlooked. It's not unusual for companies to put their website and their blog posts up first – and think about keywords much later.

The truth is, you will probably be best off hiring an SEO firm to help you get the process in place. But no SEO firm is going to be able to give you a simple formula that will magically identify the right keywords for your business and audience.

The best results are achieved when it is a collaboration between the internal experts and the SEO team. Even when I have worked with SEO experts, we've begun by interviewing key stakeholders in the company to identify the most important words or phrases. This may be the sales team, product managers, customer service staff – anyone who has exposure to customers and has insights into what they usually say when they're asking about your product or solution.

Then once we've come up with the initial list, the SEO experts can be very helpful in taking the list to the next level, to drive even better search results.

Bottom line: Your job is to balance your writing for people and for search engines.

In the old days, you'd focus on writing a killer title, introduction and balance of copy that would keep your audience engaged and get them to take an action. You were writing for a purely human audience, so it is entirely possible that your title, subhead and introduction could be written to grab the audience without any of the keywords identifying the general subject.

That is not true anymore. Writing content that you know is going to be put up on the Internet involves following a formula in which the keywords that your prospective audience tends to search for must always be found in your title and subhead, URL and also in the body copy.

This is the thing you do to make sure the search engines find your article when the humans are searching. Today's writers are no longer writing solely for humans – although your readers are the most important members you want to attract. You are now balancing your writing so that it adheres to the technical search algorithms that drive the Internet, so it can be found. Once it is found, the content must be written in a way that is understandable, useful, and interesting to the human reader.

Many product managers and marketing managers will be attracted to e-books, posts and webinars that promise to help drive Web traffic through social media, e-marketing etc.

But inevitably, most of these experts will begin and end by advising you to invest your time in writing good content that is useful to the reader. If you succeed in getting readers to the page but deliver weak content, you'll lose or offend them – driving them to someone else's site.

Twelve

Ways to Recycle and Reuse Existing Content

"Create something people want to share."

— JOHN JANTSCH

O nce content is written and published, its life is just beginning. Your life as the content manager or writer will be easier, too, if you keep the recycling opportunity in mind as you write. For one thing, smart recycling of existing content is a very efficient way to build a full content calendar. It also maximizes exposure of the content you've worked hard to create.

Following are some examples that may be of use to you.

- A 30-minute interview with a customer for a product or solution testimonial can be turned into:
    a. A one- or two-page case study that can be posted on your website

  b. A short article for your newsletter
  c. A script for a video or slideshow
  d. A success story press release
  e. A social media post with the link to the full story on your website
  f. An article submission to online magazine sites
  g. An infographic version of the success story
  h. Short quotes that can be extracted and used in other slideshows, on your website, etc
- A collection of blog posts that share practical tips can be turned into:
  a. A white paper – offered as a download in e-marketing campaigns
  b. An article for submission in industry magazines
  c. A slideshow featuring these tips for people who want a quick read
  d. Another blog post featuring the collection of tips
- A product sheet explaining the benefits of using your solution can be turned into:
  a. A slide show
  b. A newsletter article
  c. A video script featuring the product
- A white paper featuring "Six Tips to Save Money" can be turned into:
  a. Six blog posts, each featuring one of the tips

b. An infographic, if you have good enough snippets and statistics to create a compelling graphic

c. An article

d. A slideshow

e. The basis of a presentation at an industry conference

Try this with one or two pieces of content and build from there. I think you'll see how quickly it becomes second nature and how rapidly your content library can grow by taking this approach.

Thirteen

Summary

"The beautiful part of writing is that you don't have to get it right the first time, unlike, say, a brain surgeon."

— ROBERT CORMIER

I wrote this book to address a challenge that many of my clients are facing – the need to create more content, more quickly than ever, and make sure it sings with electricity and engagement. It's a tall order that requires the careful combination of creating good material and knowing how to put it to work.

The preceding chapters are intended to give you practical ideas and tools to drive ideas and manage the content generation process more efficiently. I won't say it's easy, but it's doable. It's also rewarding when you start to see your content go live.

Try a few of my suggestions and see if they make the process go a little more smoothly for you. Much of what I've shared can be learned and refined over time.

To succeed, you have to be a good writer. You have to be willing to do research. You have to be good at managing your time. Good at interviewing. Good at engaging with others to get a project done. Good at stepping back and taking an objective eye on your own work. Good at getting other people excited about what you're asking them to do.

However, when I think of all the skills it takes to be good at content generation, one top skill comes to mind. Be a good listener. If you commit to this, you'll find that your co-workers, customers and partners are a nonstop source of ideas and suggestions that can yield good content. Your challenge is to convert those ideas and suggestions into a content generation machine.

You can do it.

Author Biography

Paula Heikell is an established professional writer who has been at the forefront of content-based marketing for the last decade. She is the author of *Best Practices of the Best Dealmakers*, with Merrill Corporation and the M&A Advisor, and she co-authored *Learn to Be Lean: A Yoga-Based Approach to Healthy Weight Loss* with Shannon Leavitt, MS, RD.

Heikell holds a BS in technical communications from the University of Minnesota and provides marketing content for multiple companies. When she's not writing, she's hiking and biking her way through the mountains of New Mexico.